ORDER YOUR LIFE

MOVING GUIDE

COMPLETE MOVING GUIDE AND WORKBOOK WITH MOVING CHECKLISTS, FORMS, AND TIPS

2ND EDITION

TYWANQUILA WALKER

ISBN: 978-1-962242-00-4 (ebook)

ISBN: 978-1-962242-01-1 (paperback)

ISBN: 978-1-962242-02-8 (hardcover)

Library of Congress Control Number: 2023914727

Second Edition: October 2023

Publisher's Cataloging-in-Publication data

Names: Walker, Tywanquila, author.

Title: Order your life moving guide : complete moving guide and workbook with moving checklists , forms , and tips / by Tywanquila Walker.

Description: 2nd edition. | Millington, TN: Tywanquila Walker, 2023.

Identifiers: LCCN: 2023914727 | ISBN: 978-1-962242-02-8 (hardcover) | 978-1-962242-01-1 (paperback) | 978-1-962242-00-4 (ebook)

Subjects: LCSH Moving, Household--Handbooks, manuals, etc. | BISAC HOUSE & HOME / Moving & Relocation | HOUSE & HOME / Cleaning, Caretaking & Organizing | SELF-HELP / Self-Management / Time Management | SELF-HELP / Self-Management / Stress Management

Classification: LCC TX307 .W35 2023 | DDC 648/.9--dc23

orderyourlife.com

For More Information on How to Get (and stay)
Organized Visit
ORDERYOURLIFE.COM

CONTENTS

THE POWER OF ORGANIZATION

If you could magically pack all your belongings and transport them to where they need to be, would you do it? If your movers could psychically connect with you and know where you wanted them to put your boxes, would you allow it? If there were a way to order your life, would you accept it?

I am not a magician. I am not psychic. I do not specialize in teleportation. I am a professional organizer. I can help you find order in chaos. I can help you harness the power of organization.

I started Order Your Life because I feel your frustration. I have experienced your pain. Moving is a pain. Directing movers is a pain. Trying to find your stuff after you move is a pain. Getting your house in order is a pain.

In the United States, more than 35 million people move every year. Among that number are 6 million college-aged adults, 7 million job seekers, and 650 thousand military personnel, all transferring to new locations throughout the world. Whether they are moving or staying put, millions of people make annual resolutions to get organized and reorganize their lives.

That's a lot of movement. That's a lot of pain. That is why I'm here.

A little bit of organization goes a long way in easing the pain of chaos. You still have to do the work. Yet you can begin enjoying the sweet fruits of your labor sooner.

My mission is to help you on your journey.
There is power in organization.
Harness your power.
Order Your Life.

Tywanquila Walker, CEO & Founder of Order Your Life

MOVING:
THE BASICS
(AND THE NOT SO BASIC)

IS MOVING MORE STRESSFUL THAN JAIL?

Let's play a game.

Would you rather…?

    A. Move

    B. Plan a Wedding

    C. Go to Jail

The Results Are In…

In a survey of 2000 Americans, Life Storage and OnePoll found that 1 in 10 Americans think moving is more stressful than spending a week in jail. Yes, you read that right.

Max Knoblauch wrote a *New York Post* article titled "One in Ten Americans Would Prefer a Week in Jail Over Moving." The article includes an infographic and mentions how many happy/sad cries people experience while moving. (The number is two, in case you're wondering.)

Believe it or not, some people would prefer an orange jumpsuit over a pile of moving boxes.

How about you? What would you choose?

Since you're reading this book, I'm guessing you chose moving.

RENTER'S SECURITY DEPOSIT: MOVING IN AND OUT OF YOUR HOME

Do you remember how you felt when you first saw your home? Were you happy, sad, pleased, disappointed, or simply relieved to find a place to rent? You've had some wonderful times in that old place. Now it's time to say goodbye.

Goodbyes are always hard. Luckily, this goodbye comes with a great parting gift – your security deposit. You handed over your money to seal the renter's deal. Well, the honeymoon is over. Let me tell you how to get your money back.

Move In Inspection

When you moved into your home, you probably had to complete a move in inspection. The move in inspection shows that the property was in good order when you arrived. Rental property inspections protect landlords and allow them to charge for damages to the property. Inspections also protect you from being charged for damages that existed before you moved in.

Completing a detailed property inspection seems like a hassle when you're trying to move all of your stuff into your new home. However, this inspection is important if you want to get your deposit back when you move out.

The first step is to be thorough during your move in inspection. Take pictures of your home when you move in. Note all damages, including holes, chipped paint, dirty appliances, broken appliances, missing light fixtures and window screens, ripped carpet, leaky faucets, and broken doors. No detail is too small. Use the *Order Your Life Move In/Out Inspection Form* if your landlord or rental manager did not give you an inspection form.

Yes, your landlord will probably be annoyed with you for being so meticulous. Ignore the annoyance. Completing this form is in your best interest. For example, there is a stain on the living room wall when you move in. You don't note the stain on your move in inspection. When you move out, the landlord notices the stain and tells you the wall needs to be repainted. Not a problem, right? Not necessarily. The money to repaint may come out of your deposit.

If your landlord was already planning to paint when you moved out, you probably won't be charged for a small stain. However, I once had a rental manager try to charge me for a nonexistent stain. He walked through the empty apartment with me on move out day. He told me everything was perfect (and I know it was because I'd cleaned like crazy). The rental company had a policy that they painted every time someone moved out. I used my move in inspection, and the pictures, to show that I had not damaged the apartment. After a few meetings and some emails, I finally got my entire deposit back.

After I moved out, I discovered that charging for painting was a common tactic of this rental manager. He didn't want to pay for paint out of his own budget, so he routinely told tenants they'd damaged the property and needed to pay for repairs. Unfortunately, many of the former tenants were too busy to haggle with this manager and get their money back. Even with evidence, I had a hard time. The honeymoon was definitely over.

Move Out Inspection

The process for moving out is very similar to the process for moving in. Take pictures of everything. Make note of everything.

As soon as you know you're moving out, start cleaning and making repairs. Contact maintenance immediately. Ask them to do repairs. Generally, if maintenance does the repairs while you are a tenant, you won't be charged. Keep in mind that maintenance crews usually do small repairs caused by normal wear and tear (e.g., fixing leaky faucets, replacing old appliances, and fixing that oven that keeps breaking down).

If you have severely damaged the home (e.g., holes in the walls, broken doors or windows, or ripped flooring), you will have to pay for those damages. If your home is dirty or in need of repair when you move out, be prepared to forfeit some, or all, of your deposit.

It may work in your favor to hire a cleaning crew. Some rental agencies have a preferred cleaning company and guarantee return of your deposit if you hire them to clean the home. Ask your landlord or rental manager about cleaning company options.

How do you get your deposit back? Leave your rental home as good as or better than you found it.

Schedule a move out inspection with your landlord or rental manager. Schedule the inspection for a time when you know the home will be empty and clean. Get the move out inspection date and time in writing.

Ask your landlord or rental manager for a move out checklist. If they do not have a move out checklist, use the *Order Your Life Move In/Out Inspection Form*.

Before the move out inspection, make sure all of your belongings are off the property. Landlords will charge you if they have to remove trash or personal property from the rental home. Check your lease for move out terms and conditions. You don't want to receive any surprises (i.e., surprise charges) after you've moved out.

During your move out inspection, go through the checklist as you walk through the property. Make notes. If there are damages, ask about costs and whether you will receive your entire deposit. If everything is fine, get confirmation in writing.

At the end of the inspection, have your landlord or rental manager sign and date the checklist. If the landlord or rental manager wants to keep the checklist, ask for a copy of the checklist, or take a picture of it with your cell phone. Keep the checklist with your moving documents.

How long should you keep your lease and inspection paperwork? At the very least, keep your paperwork until you receive your deposit. Save the documents even longer if you suspect you will need them later (or if you like to keep documents "just in case"). Scan the documents, or use a mobile app, and save them electronically.

The New Honeymoon

You can follow the old adage, "Always leave a place better than you found it." Or you can subscribe to the motto, "It's mine and I want it back."

Either way, leave your rental home clean and tidy. Get your money back. Then prepare to embark on a new honeymoon filled with pictures, detailed notes, and an adventurous happily ever after.

Here is your honeymoon guide: *Order Your Life Move In/Out Inspection Form.*

Use the *Apartment and House Hunting Checklist* to compare honeymoon destinations.

Enjoy!

MOVING BOXES: HOW MANY DO I NEED?

When moving, one of the trickiest variables to determine is the number of boxes you will need. Large quantities of boxes and bins are expensive, and difficult to store. However, they are necessities that you cannot ignore during your move.

Before your move, you will need to go to the store to buy boxes, order them online, or scour your neighborhood stores for sturdy, free boxes. You may even be able to get boxes from someone who has recently moved. No matter how you get your boxes, it is critical for you to assess how many you will need to effectively carry out your move. Think about it. Would you rather figure out how many boxes you need now, then spend one (or two) efforts gathering them all? Or would you rather make multiple trips to the store, submit more online orders, or keep showing up in the back alley of your favorite store?

Moving is one of the few times when it's okay to have more than you need. Having too many boxes is much better than not having enough. If you order boxes in store or online, check the return policy. You may be able to return unused boxes. If your boxes were free or you do not want to return them, pass them along to a friend or neighbor, recycle them, sell or exchange them online, or donate them to a charity (e.g., one that packs foods or ships items).

Based on the square footage of your home, the number of rooms in it, and the number of people who live with you, it is possible to estimate the number of boxes you will need for your move. As you read, think about whether you are a bit of a collector or more of a minimalist. Increase or decrease your box estimate accordingly.

Visualize yourself packing and determine how many large boxes you need. As a general rule of thumb, you should pack light, bulky items (e.g., comforters and towels) in large boxes and heavy, dense items (e.g., books) in smaller boxes. The size and weight of the box is important.

Someone has to carry each box. A large box full of books is unwieldy and very difficult to carry.

Studio Apartments

Depending on the location, studios can vary widely in size. However, in the United States, studio apartments are generally between 500 and 600 square feet.

If you live in a studio apartment, purchase between 10 and 20 boxes in preparation for your move. Err on the side of caution and purchase 20 small to medium boxes as opposed to 10 large ones. At the end of the packing process, you don't want to end up packing fragile items with heavy, bulky items because you only have one large box left to put things in.

Keep in mind that the number of boxes you need increases as the size of your household increases. While 20 small boxes may suffice for a single person in a studio, for two people, you may need between 25 and 35 boxes.

If using a combination of large, medium, and small boxes, plan your packing. Do you have enough items for all those large boxes? Or will smaller boxes suffice?

1 to 2 Bedrooms

As with studios, the number of boxes needed for a 1- to 2-bedroom home will depend on the number of people in the household.

- For one adult living in a 1-bedroom home, 35 to 40 small to medium boxes and 1 to 2 large boxes should suffice.

- Two people living in a 2-bedroom home will need between 50 and 60 small to medium boxes and 2 to 4 large boxes.

- Two adults and 1 child will need an estimated 70 small to medium boxes and 4 to 6 large boxes.

- Two adults with 2 children will need around 75 small to medium boxes and 4 to 8 large boxes.

Using larger boxes may decrease the number of boxes you will need. For example, for a two-person household, consider using 6 large boxes, 30 medium boxes, and 15 small boxes. That's a total of 51 boxes.

As mentioned above, be mindful of the weight of the boxes. It is preferable to have 3 small boxes that can be easily moved as opposed to one large box that is impossible to lift.

3+ Bedrooms

One variable to consider is how modestly you live. Your lifestyle will greatly affect the number of boxes you need. Households with 3 or more bedrooms typically house a lot of belongings. Three or more people usually live in the home, and each have their own personal possessions.

For a large 3-bedroom home with multiple occupants, 80 to 100 small to medium boxes and 4 to 8 large boxes are needed. For each additional adult, add 10 to 20 boxes. For each additional child, add 5 to 10 boxes.

Do you have an attic, basement, shed, or garage? Factor in how many boxes you need to pack the items in these areas. The more stuff you have, the more boxes you will need.

General Estimates by Room Type

In addition to the size of the home, the type of room you are packing offers some insight into how many boxes you need. Below are some general estimates of the number of boxes you will need for each room.

As always, be mindful of how much stuff you have. More stuff equals more boxes.

Estimated Number of Boxes Needed Per Room

Room	Small	Medium	Large	Extra Large	Wardrobe	Dish	Total
Bedroom (Adult)	7	6	4	1	4	--	22
Bedroom (Child Over 12)	6	5	3	1	3	--	18
Bedroom (Child Under 12)	4	5	3	1	2	--	15
Bathroom	2	2	2	--	--	--	6
Kitchen	4	6	3	--	--	5	18
Dining Room	2	2	1	--	--	3	8
Living Room	5	5	3	--	--	2	15
Office	8	3	1	--	--	1	13

Box Sizes

Small box – 1.5 cubic feet

Medium box – 3 cubic feet

Large box – 4.5 cubic feet

Extra large box – 6 cubic feet

Wardrobe box – 10 cubic feet

Dish box – 1.85 to 5 cubic feet

Adult Bedrooms

Adult bedrooms are typically master bedrooms or the largest bedrooms in the home. Larger rooms tend to house more items and larger objects. As a result, each adult should allot several small, medium, and large boxes for moving. Pack small items such as jewelry and accessories in small boxes. In medium boxes, pack electronics, clothes, and shoes. In large and extra large boxes, pack bulky items such as comforters, pillows, and linens. Hang clothes in wardrobe boxes. In addition to boxes, use suitcases, duffle bags, and backpacks to pack your items.

Children's Bedrooms (Under 12)

Children under 12 have a surprisingly long list of inventory. Pack large items (e.g., large toys, playsets, and blankets) in large and extra large boxes. Use medium boxes for clothes and medium sized toys. Reserve small boxes for small plush toys, miniature cars, small building blocks, and collector sets.

For items that are part of a set (e.g., puzzles and toy sets), pack the sets in individual small boxes; then, place the small boxes inside a larger box. "Double boxing" will help you keep the sets together while reducing the number of individual boxes that have to be loaded onto the moving truck.

For children between the ages of 6 and 12, use wardrobe boxes to hang shirts, sweaters, and other large clothing items.

Children's Bedrooms (Over 12)

Like their younger counterparts, children over 12 have a large inventory of items. While their need for boxes may be lesser than adults', large boxes are needed to pack large electronics (e.g., televisions and computers), large toys, and sports equipment. Use medium and large boxes for linens, curtains, and art supplies. Pack comforters and blankets in extra large boxes. Pack gaming systems in sturdy small and medium sized boxes. Pack personal items and clothes in wardrobe boxes.

Bathrooms

Compared to the rest of the home, bathrooms are relatively empty. For each bathroom in your home, use 2 small, 2 medium, and 2 large boxes. The large boxes are for towels, linens, and bathmats. Pack toiletries, bottles, cleaning supplies, soap dishes, and small bathroom accessories in the small and medium boxes. Tightly secure all lids and caps and tape them closed. As added protection against leaks, put liquids in plastic bags or zip bags. If there is a leak, the bags will protect your other items from damage.

Kitchens and Dining Rooms

Kitchens and dining rooms demand a little more diversity in terms of types of boxes. There are large items (e.g., appliances) and small items (e.g., silverware). In large and medium boxes, pack pots, pans, and appliances such as microwaves, blenders, and toaster ovens. Use medium boxes for dishware, linens, and cooking equipment. Pack forks, knives, linen napkins, and dining accessories in small boxes.

For breakables such as china, dishes, crystal, and glassware, use dish boxes. Dish boxes are double-walled extra strength boxes with dividers or partitions. Dish boxes come in a variety of sizes, and are designed to protect dishes and glassware.

Living Rooms and Offices

Similar to the kitchen and dining room, you will need a variety of boxes to pack your living room and office. Pack books, lamps, figurines, small decorations, and small portraits in small and medium boxes. Use picture boxes (also called mirror boxes) for mirrors, paintings, artwork, large portraits, and framed posters. Carefully pack your flat screen television in a TV box. Pack electronics in small and medium boxes.

If you have a large number of files, pack your files in document storage boxes. Document boxes can be used with or without hanging file folders, and they will ensure your files stay organized during your move.

When in Doubt, Ask for Help

For additional guidance on your moving box needs, contact a moving company and ask a moving professional for help. A professional mover will do a survey of your home and provide you with a written estimate of the number and types of boxes you will need. The estimate is called an inventory, or cube sheet. The inventory will list each room, items in the rooms, number and types of boxes needed, and an estimated weight of the items. The inventory is free. It is part of the process of providing a moving quote.

If a company refuses to conduct an inventory, or refuses to give you a cost estimate, contact another company. A professional mover will listen to you and answer your questions. A professional mover will also provide you with an inventory sheet and a price quote, because it is standard practice in the moving industry.

Whether you are a minimalist or a collector, I wish you the best of luck with your move.

Still have questions? Check out the *Order Your Life Moving Checklist* for a detailed moving timeline and guide.

5 QUESTIONS TO ASK A POTENTIAL MOVING COMPANY

If you are searching for a moving company, you have probably scoured the web and read countless customer reviews. Well done! Doing your research is an important step in finding a moving company that is right for you.

After you find your top three candidates, ask each moving company questions that will help you spot red flags and determine which company will earn the right to move your belongings.

Begin by asking these five questions.

1. Can you give me an in-home, written estimate?

The moving company should be willing to send a representative to your home. The representative should provide you with a written estimate of moving costs and time. If the moving company is unwilling to conduct a moving inspection and provide a written estimate, that is a red flag. Continue searching for a reputable company.

2. Are you insured? What kind of insurance do you have?

The company should be willing to provide you their insurance information. They should be able to tell you what kind of insurance the company has, what the insurance covers, and any limitations of the coverage. If a moving company does not have insurance, it is unlikely they will we able to cover any loses or damages that may happen during your move.

3. How many movers will you send for this job?

Evaluate the moving company's manpower and planning. The moving company representative should be able to tell you how many people it will take to move your belongings. An experienced representative can estimate how many people it will take to complete your moving job. The representative may also be able tell you who usually works on the day you are planning to move. If the representative cannot give you a clear answer, it is possible they do not know the company's schedule or how many people are on staff.

4. Who do I contact if I have questions, or if there are problems, the day of the move?

The moving company should provide you with the contact information of someone who will be available on the day of your move. There should be a manager, representative, or office staff member available to take your call during your move. If you encounter a problem, first, try to resolve the problem with the moving crew leader or foreman. If you are unable to resolve the problem with the crew, someone in a managerial position should be able to help you.

5. Are your movers full-time employees?

Given that moving companies often hire part-time or temporary employees during the peak of moving season, this question is optional. However, if you can determine the moving company's composition of full-time employees, part-time employees, and independent contractors, you may be able to ascertain the reliability of the moving crew. Compared to a company that randomly (and temporarily) hires anyone who is available, a company with steady staff may have a more dependable moving crew. The moving company's response regarding their employees provides insight into the company's hiring practices and how they select their moving crew. Established moving companies usually have full-time and part-time employees who have worked with them for years.

Finding a good moving company doesn't have to be difficult. Do your research and ask as many questions as necessary before making a decision.

HIGH VALUE INVENTORY

In the moving industry, an item worth more than $100 per pound* is a high value item. We often think of antiques, collectibles, jewelry, and electronics as high value items. And they are. However, don't forget about expensive shoes and clothes, computer software, furniture, musical instruments, and important documents.

When you purchase insurance coverage from your mover, most moving companies will ask you to declare all high value items on an inventory form. Without this form, movers are only liable for $100 per pound per article. What does that mean? It means if you bought a 2-pound purse for $500, the moving company is only liable for $200 (i.e., 2 pounds x $100 = $200). What about your extensive video game collection? Or all those comic books you've had since childhood? Yep. Those are probably high value items.

It is in your best interest to complete a high value inventory form. The form helps you, and the movers, identify high value items. Movers usually take very good care of high value inventory. They use the form to make sure your items are delivered in good condition.

*Note: The definition of a high value item varies across moving companies. For example, some companies do not use the per pound measure. Instead, items worth more than $1000 are considered high value items. Ask your moving company representative how the moving company defines high value items.

Are There Any Guarantees?

Although the form is an inventory of items worth more than $100 per pound, it does not guarantee you will receive the full value of the item when you make an insurance claim. When you make a claim, you must state the amount of the claim. For example, a desk you bought for $1000 is scratched during the move. It is unlikely you will make a claim for $1000, or that the moving company will pay a $1000 claim. Instead, you may ask for $50 to repair the scratch.

Additionally, the high value inventory form does not provide proof of the item's actual value. Before you move, get high value items appraised. For items that are not appraised, track down your receipts and make note of the purchase price of the items. Keep your receipts in one place (e.g., scan them and email them to yourself, print them and seal them in an envelope, make pdfs and save them on your computer). You may only have days after your move to file a claim. Don't waste time searching for receipts. Familiarize yourself with your moving company's policies and procedures for making insurance and damaged property claims.

You probably won't get the original value for the item, but you may receive the purchase price minus depreciation (i.e., what the item is worth after subtracting the cost of wear, tear, and age). You may also receive replacement costs (i.e., what it would cost to buy the item today). For example, 10 years ago, you bought the latest model television for $1000. Today, you can get a similar television for $250. The moving company may only honor a claim for $250. Is this fair? Probably. A 10-year-old television has seen a lot of wear and tear, and a similar television bought today costs much less than $1000.

Listing items on a high value inventory form does not mean the items are fully covered. Even if the moving company provided the form, completing a high value inventory form does not guarantee your items are insured. Ask your mover about insurance coverage options and costs. Get information about insurance coverage in writing. Make sure you understand your options.

Filing an Insurance Claim

When you file a claim, use your judgement to decide what the items or repairs are worth. Do not be surprised if the moving company makes a counter offer for your claim amount. If you do not accept the counter offer, you may have to provide a written explanation for why you should get more money for that item. Use your receipts, appraisal values, and before and after pictures to justify your claim.

You should also file claims for damaged items that are not listed on the high value inventory form. For example, you bought 4 plates for $12. A mover dropped the box and you now have a box full of broken plates. File a claim for the plates. Although the items are not high value, the moving company is liable for the property damage.

Check and Double Check

Whether you purchase coverage through your moving company or not, always list your items on a high value inventory form. Use the form to keep track of your high value items before and after the move. When you arrive at your new home, make sure you account for your items before the movers leave. Check and double check.

If possible, transport high value items yourself. Keep them within sight to make sure they arrive safely at your new home. Take pictures of your items, record serial numbers, and write detailed descriptions so you can identify the items if they are lost or damaged during your move.

If your moving company has a high value inventory form, use the company's form. Otherwise, use the *Order Your Life High Value Inventory Form*.

See *Non-Allowables: Items Not Allowed on Moving Trucks* for more information about high value items and personal possessions.

PEOPLE TO NOTIFY WHEN I MOVE:
CHANGE OF ADDRESS

You've started packing. You've scouted out your new neighborhood. You've called the moving company three times to make sure they arrive on time. You've even told your family and friends your new address. Good job! Have you forgotten anything?

Did you contact the post office or change your address online? Did you ask your doctor to forward your medical records? Did you contact your internet provider to cancel or reroute your service?

In the chaos of moving, it's easy to forget about all the people you need to notify of your move. From your employer to the DMV, the list of people who need to know can be daunting.

Don't worry, Order Your Life has a checklist to help you remember who to contact.

Step 1, change your address online with the United States Postal Service (USPS). Go to https://moversguide.usps.com to complete the online form. You can get your mail forwarded for up to 1 year.

Step 2, use the *People to Notify When I Move Checklist*. The checklist is broken down into categories to make the process easier.

MOVING WITH CHILDREN

Moving is a stressful time for adults and children alike. While adults are busy organizing, planning, and preparing for the future, children are busy trying to make sense of the changes, thinking about the friends they'll leave behind, and wondering what their new lives will be like.

Whether you're moving across the country or two blocks away, a move disrupts your family routine. Change is scary for adults. Change is scary for children, especially when they are not involved in the moving process.

Get Your Children Involved

If your child is having a difficult time, think about the situation from your child's perspective.

- Does your child understand why your family is moving?
- Was your child involved in the decision to move?
- Has your child ever moved before?
- Has your child moved many times?
- What is your child afraid to leave behind? Friends? A teacher? A youth club or sports team? A favorite park or zoo?
- Will your child know people at your new home?
- Will your child easily make new friends?
- Will everyone in your household move with your child?
- What will your child miss most about your old home?

As you know, moving involves more than simply packing your bags and showing up at a new location. We have emotional ties to people and things. Even when we know something better awaits us, change is hard. Moving is hard.

One of the best ways to make moving easier for children is to get them involved in the process. Your children may not be happy about the move. You may even encounter resistance, but your children will at least know what's going on. Being involved and knowing what's happening may lessen your children's anxiety.

It's Time to Talk

Be positive and reassuring throughout the move. Talk about the move. If possible, let your children help you plan house-hunting trips, search for new schools, visit your new home, and explore the new neighborhood. Assign moving responsibilities so they feel part of the move. For example, let your children pack their toys and personal belongings. Let them decorate their boxes. Let them know their roles and responsibilities are important.

Give children as much information as you can as soon as you can. Tell them about their new home. Tell them when you plan to move. Show them pictures of their new home and school.

Answer your children's questions honestly. If you don't know the answer to a question, let your children help you find the answer. For example, if your child wants to know if there is a park where you're going, search a map to find the park nearest your new home. If there is not a park nearby, point out other fun places like a lake, sports stadium, library, or museum. Help your children find the positives. Assure them that you are listening to their concerns. Involve them in planning their new lives.

Patience, Patience, Patience

Your children may need special attention and lots of reassurance. Be patient with them.

If your children are very young (e.g., toddlers or preschoolers), they may not be able to tell you what's bothering them. Their fear and anxiety may be expressed as clinginess, or they may exhibit regression of some developmental milestones (e.g., sleeping and toilet training). They may need a few extra hugs and kisses. Be generous with your compassion.

They are just as worried as you, although they can't tell you that.

If your children are older (e.g., in elementary school, adolescents, or teenagers), they may not want to tell you what's bothering them. Their fear and anxiety may be expressed as anger. They may need a few extra hugs and kisses. Be generous with your compassion. They are just as worried as you, although they won't tell you that.

The Knowledge Continues

For more tips to help make your child's move easier, read *Tips for Moving with Children.*

Also check out *Moving Books for You and Your Child.*

MOVING WITH PETS

When you arrive home from a long day at work, Snuggles, Hugs, and Kisses are waiting for you. They love you. They're happy to see you. They want dinner right now.

Snuggles, Hugs, and Kisses aren't nicknames for your significant other (aka Cutie Pie). SH&K are your pets. They're those adorable little creatures who show you unconditional love and support.

When you start making plans to move, SH&K will notice. They are sensitive to changes in their environment. In addition to seeing boxes slowly pile up around your home, SH&K will pick up on changes in your mood and stress level.

Granted, if SH&K are fish or reptiles, they may swim and slither along in complete oblivion, ignoring your boxes. However, if SH&K are four-legged, furry, or feathered, your mood becomes their mood. Your stress becomes their stress.

Although some pets are more sensitive to pre-move planning than others, during a move, all pets have the potential to become stressed. Whether they have wings, scales, fur, or feathers, take care of your pets as you move them from your old home to your new home. Try not to stress them out. Provide them with the support they need to move safely. Show Snuggles, Hugs, and Kisses how much you love them.

For ways to share the love, read *Tips for Moving with Pets*. There are tips for dogs, cats, birds, fish, reptiles, horses, and small pets such as hamsters, gerbils, and rabbits.

CHECKLISTS

ORDER YOUR LIFE MOVING CHECKLIST

Moving is a complex process, one that demands time, energy, and patience from everyone involved. One of the best ways to facilitate moving is to prepare as thoroughly as possible. Prepare well in advance. Then execute your plans meticulously.

The detailed checklist below begins 8 weeks before moving and ends the day after your move. If possible, begin making plans even earlier than 8 weeks prior to moving, as you may (and probably will) need to make adjustments for unexpected situations.

Week 8

Begin making preparations to move. Determine what you will need to make your move go smoothly.

- ❑ Make a moving folder. Keep all of your moving documents, receipts, notes, and lists in the folder. Consider getting a folder in a bright color so it stands apart from your other files.

- ❑ Notify your property owner that you intend to move.

    - ❑ If you are renting, check your lease to make sure you give written notice in a timely fashion (e.g., 30 or 60 days before moving). Give notice on month-to-month rent, either verbally or in writing, depending on the terms of your lease and any agreements you made with the landlord or rental manager.

    - ❑ If you sold your home, clarify move out terms with your real estate agent and/or the new homeowners. Check your written contract for specific move out terms and conditions.

- ❑ Get on-site estimates from at least 3 moving companies.

    - ❑ Scout out moving companies or moving truck rental agencies that will fit your needs. If possible, meet with company representatives. Read online reviews. Ask friends and family for referrals. Know what you're getting before you give them money.

- ❑ Get the estimates in writing. Do not rely on over-the-phone or online estimates. How do they know what to charge if they haven't seen your stuff?

- ❑ Compare and contrast the moving companies. Keep in mind that the company with the lowest price may not be the company that best suits your needs.

- ❑ Safety Tip: Know the name of the moving representative who is coming to your house. If you will be home alone, always contact a family member or neighbor so someone knows who is stopping by your house. You can even stay on the phone until the mover gets there then say, for example, "Hey, Mom. *Mover X* is here. I'll call you back after I get the estimate." You can also send a friend a text when the representative arrives and another text when the representative leaves. Every moving representative I've met has been courteous and professional. However, I still let someone know a moving representative is stopping by to give me an estimate.

❑ Make logistical arrangements.

- ❑ Order, buy, or consider renting equipment that may prove necessary during your move. Do you need trucks, moving dollies, or portable moving containers?

- ❑ If you are moving yourself, think about friends and family members who can help you move. Are they available? Do they have equipment you can use? Do you need to pay them (in pizza or in cash)?

Week 7

Direct your attention towards inventory. Visualize your new home and assess what furniture and items will be moved.

- ❑ Go through every room in your home, take inventory, and determine what you want to keep and what you want to get rid of.
    - ❑ Determine what needs to be sold, donated, given away, or thrown away.
    - ❑ Sort, purge, and get rid of items you no longer need.
- ❑ Gather large bins or boxes and label them "sell", "donate", "give away", and "keep".
    - ❑ If you plan to have a garage sale, set the date, apply for a permit from your city, and put all of your garage sale items in a designated space.
    - ❑ As soon as your donate bin is full, take it to the donation center.
    - ❑ As soon as you identify an item that needs to be given away, give it away. Sit your give aways by the front door to take with you the next time you leave the house, or put them in your car.
    - ❑ If an item needs to be thrown away, toss it immediately.
    - ❑ Do not let your bins sit around for weeks and take up space; you will need that space when you begin packing.
- ❑ Visualize your new home.
    - ❑ If possible, measure all of the rooms in your new home. Measure the furniture that you will be moving. Use graph paper, a computer program, or paper and a ruler to make a scaled layout of your new home. Include doors, closets, windows, and furniture.
    - ❑ Make copies of your layout. You will need to give a copy

of your layout to the movers and post it in your new home on moving day.

Week 6

Order moving and packing supplies. Get everyone involved in the moving and packing process. Consider storage options. Pack items that will be placed in storage.

- ❑ Purchase moving boxes, packing supplies, and an Order Your Life Moving Kit (https://orderyourlife.com/collections/moving-labels).

  - ❑ Get tape, bubble wrap, and permanent markers.

  - ❑ Think about how many boxes you will need for your move. For guidance on type and number of boxes, read *Moving Boxes: How Many Do I Need?*

- ❑ Assign each member of your household a set of responsibilities during the next few weeks. For example, give children the responsibility of boxing their toys and packing their personal items. Let them decorate their boxes and involve them in the moving process. For more ideas about how to get your children involved, see *Moving with Children, Tips for Moving with Children,* and *Moving Books for You and Your Child.*

- ❑ If necessary, consider storage options for items you want to keep but will not be moving into your new home.

  - ❑ Consider the cost of storage. How long will the items be stored? What are the storage rental fees? Will you need special equipment to move these items to a storage facility? Will it be more cost-effective to sell or donate your items instead of storing them?

  - ❑ Visit storage facilities. Check out storage options to make sure they are appropriate for your needs. What size room do you need? Does the facility need to be climate controlled?

❏ Move items into storage as soon as possible. Move items to the storage facility on one day and move items to your new home on a different day. Consider them as two separate moves. Getting items mixed up or placed in the wrong location will complicate your move.

Week 5

Pack nonessential items. Polish up your current place and notify service providers of your impending move.

❏ Begin packing items that you will move to your new home.

❏ Start by packing your nonessential items and things that you rarely use.

❏ Pack books, nonessential dishware, extra linens, decorating accessories, paintings, seasonal decorations, and other home goods that you do not use every day.

❏ Pack out-of-season clothes. For example, if you are moving during the summer, pack your winter gear.

❏ Make note of valuable items.

❏ Do these items require additional insurance during your move?

❏ Take pictures of your items, record serial numbers, and write detailed descriptions so that you can identify the items if they are lost or damaged during your move.

❏ To learn more about high value items, read *High Value Inventory*. Record information about these items on the *Order Your Life High Value Inventory Form*.

❏ Label your boxes. Clear labeling will make it easy for you to find boxes after your move.

❏ If you have the space, designate a packing room. The packing room is where you store all of your packed boxes and packing supplies. By assigning a packing room, you can have a dedicated packing space while continuing to live comfortably in the rest of your home.

❑ If you do not have the space for a packing room, assign a corner of a room as a designated packing space. Neatly place packed boxes in that corner. Do not obstruct passageways or entryways. Depending on the configuration of your home, you may want to assign a packing corner for each room.

❑ Take a walk through your home and make note of any areas that need to be repaired. This is especially important for renters, as damage to the home may affect the return of your deposit.

  ❑ Do walls need to be spackled? Does painting need to be retouched? Can you do the repairs yourself, or should you call maintenance?

  ❑ If you (or maintenance) can do the work for little or no cost, get the work completed well before you move out. Otherwise, be prepared to forfeit a portion of your deposit.

❑ Notify your service providers that you will be moving. Companies you should contact include internet, phone, cable, and satellite providers; electric, water, gas, sewage, and waste companies; and lawn care and snow removal companies.

  ❑ Check how much service and coverage you will have in your new home. For example, is the cell phone, cable, and internet coverage enough to meet your family's needs? If necessary, research service providers near your new home.

  ❑ If you are keeping the service, notify the service provider of your change of address. Provide dates for when you want service disconnected at your old address and when you want service reconnected at your new address.

  ❑ If you no longer need the service, set up a cancellation date and ask about cancellation fees and policies.

- ❑ If you will need new services, or services from a different company, contact the service providers and schedule dates to connect the services at your new home.

❑ Make a list of other companies or agencies that you will need to notify regarding your change of address. For example, you will want to contact your bank, your doctor, schools, and the postal service. See the *People to Notify When I Move Checklist*. Also read *People to Notify When I Move: Change of Address*.

❑ Scan or make copies of all of your important documents. Store your documents in a safe place.

- ❑ Consider how you will transport your documents. Do you need a safe box? Will you transport the documents in your personal vehicle?

- ❑ Make sure a family member or friend knows where to find the documents if there is an emergency.

- ❑ If you do not want to scan or copy your documents, consider using a mobile app for electronic backup. Check the security settings of the app and use caution when uploading information. For example, you may not want to save personal, financial, or legal information on the app. Make sure you know the security level of the app as well as how your information will be stored and used. Only use apps from trusted sources.

❑ If necessary, make hotel and travel arrangements.

- ❑ If you are moving a long distance, make sure you book your hotel room, airline tickets, and other transportation well in advance.

- ❑ If you are staying with friends or family, let them know your travel plans.

Week 4

Continue packing and minimize your purchases. Determine if you need to make special arrangements for work or school. Consider the needs of your pets.

- ❑ Continue packing and labeling your boxes. Space out your packing to make the task more manageable.

    - ❑ Each day, designate time for organizing and packing.

    - ❑ An hour or two of packing each day means you will be less likely to spend the entire day before your move (or the day of your move) packing.

- ❑ Limit your purchase of perishable items, bulk foods, or bulk supplies that will not be moved to your new home.

- ❑ Begin eating, or discarding, perishable foods that you do not want to move.

- ❑ Donate canned goods or other food items.

- ❑ Use up items that you do not want to move (e.g., cleaning supplies) or items that your moving company will not transport (e.g., flammable or hazardous materials). Ask your moving company about items that they will not transport. Also see *Non-Allowables: Items Not Allowed on Moving Trucks.*

- ❑ Notify your employer, your school, or your children's school or daycare about your move. Do you need to request days off work during your move? Do you need to notify your children's school, daycare, or bus driver? Do you need to make special childcare arrangements during your move?

- ❑ Do you have a family member with special needs? Do you need to make special arrangements for a family member during your move? Do you need to make special arrangements for medical supplies? How will you move your family member from your old home to your new home?

- ❑ Consider how you will move your pets to your new home. Do you need to make special pet sitting arrangements? For tips and pet moving guidance, read *Moving with Pets* and *Tips for Moving with Pets*.

Week 3

Pack nonessential furniture and small appliances. Organize your items and make them easier to move.

❑ Disassemble nonessential furniture.

    ❑ Pack bookcases, side tables, lamps, and other items that will not be needed regularly over the next 3 weeks. Make sure you remove all lightbulbs before packing the lamps.

    ❑ Take pictures of your items so that you will know how to reassemble them. Also take pictures of the cords and setup configurations of your electronic devices.

❑ Use small, plastic zip bags to store screws, nails, and other small parts.

    ❑ Use a permanent maker to label the bags.

    ❑ On the bag, write the name of the item and the room where the item belongs.

    ❑ If possible, tape the labeled plastic zip bags to the appropriate items.

    ❑ If tape will ruin the furniture, or if the bags may fall off or rip during the move, put all of the bags in their own labeled box. Consider transporting your box of screws, nails, and small parts in your personal vehicle instead of putting it on a moving truck. You do not want to lose this box. Be sure to include the tools you'll need to reassemble the furniture.

❑ Pack small appliances such as blenders, food processors, and mixers.

❑ If you plan to use small appliances (e.g., juicers and coffee makers) and would like to pack them a few days before the move, prep the appliances so that they are move out ready.

❑ Get boxes that are the appropriate sizes for the appliances. Label the boxes to help you remember which appliance goes in each box and what room it belongs in after the move.

❑ Gather the appliance's parts and accessories in one place. If possible, pack the accessories in the labeled box.

❑ Give the appliance a thorough cleaning in preparation for your move. Packing will be easier if you only have to give the item a cursory cleaning before putting it in the box.

❑ Organize your boxes by room.

❑ For example, put all of the kitchen boxes together in a designated room or a designated corner. Put the living room boxes together.

❑ Grouping your boxes by room makes it more likely that those boxes will be placed close together on the moving truck, which will help movers put things in the right places when they are unloaded at your new home.

Week 2

Begin packing essential items and keep them within reach. Confirm arrangements with your moving company. Request a move out inspection. Take your car for a tune up.

❑ Begin packing essential items such as clothes and toiletries.

❑ These are items that you use often and will need days after your move.

❑ Keep these items within reach, as you may need them occasionally before you move.

❑ Consider packing these items in bins with sturdy,

closable lids so that you do not have to untape boxes if you discover you packed an item that you need.

❑ If you pack the items in boxes, consider waiting until the day before the move to tape them shut.

❑ Contact your moving company to confirm moving logistics (e.g., date, time, location, number of movers, and number of trucks) and costs (e.g., insurance and fees).

❑ Request a move out inspection from your landlord or rental manager.

❑ Schedule the inspection for after you have moved all of your personal belongings off the property. Give yourself time to tidy up the property after the movers are done.

❑ Ask your landlord or rental manager for a move out checklist. If they do not have a move out checklist, check your lease for move out terms and conditions. You can also use the *Order Your Life Move In/Out Inspection Form.*

❑ Get the move out inspection date and time in writing.

❑ Take your vehicle for a tune up.

❑ This is especially important if you are moving far away and will be driving your vehicle to your new home.

❑ If you are moving to a different climate, consider which car services you might need. For example, do you need new tires, better windshield wipers, or special car accessories?

Week 1

Pack your suitcases. Pack an "open first" box. Refill your prescriptions.

❑ Pack a suitcase for everyone in your family.

❑ Pack items that you use every day and will need immediately after your move.

❑ Include enough clothes and toiletries for the next few

days.

- ❑ Pack a few toys, books, or games for your children to keep them entertained during or after the move.
- ❑ Pack toys and food for your pets.

❑ Transport your suitcases in your personal vehicle instead of putting them on a moving truck. If this is not possible, load your suitcases onto the moving truck last. As soon as you arrive at your new home, unload the suitcases and put them in a location that will be easy to access after the truck is unpacked.

❑ Pack an "open first" box.

- ❑ Pack a box that contains essential things you will need after your move.
- ❑ Write "Open First" on the box.
- ❑ Possible open first box items include plates, cups, utensils, a pot or pan, a can opener, a coffee pot or kettle, snacks, nonperishable foods, toiletries, and cleaning supplies.
- ❑ Think about the things you use every day and have yet to pack. Chances are some of these items should go in your open first box.
- ❑ Consider using a clear bin with a lid as your open first box. The box will be easier to find and you will be able to see exactly what's inside.

❑ As with your suitcases, consider transporting your open first box in your personal vehicle. If this is not possible, your open first box should be one of the last items loaded onto the truck and one of the first that is unloaded. Put your box in an easy to access location.

❑ Refill your prescriptions.

- ❑ Refill prescriptions that you will need during the next few weeks.

❑ Make a list of your medications and store everything in one place.

❑ Pack essential medicines in your suitcase for easy access.

❑ Consider how you will store medicines with specific requirements. For example, do you need a cooler to keep the medicine cold during the move?

❑ Consider whether you will need to take medication during your move. Where will you store it? When, and how often, will you take it? Do you need to take your medication with food or water?

❑ As a precaution, check the pharmacies near your new home to make sure they accept your insurance. Give this information to your prescribing provider or doctor, as you may need to fill a prescription during an emergency or unexpected illness.

❑ Contact your service providers. Confirm that your services will be disconnected at your old address and reconnected at your new address. Verify the dates.

❑ Make arrangements to pick up the keys to your new home. Will someone meet you at your new home? Is there a lock box on the front door? Do you have the combination to the lock box?

❑ Pack nonperishable food that you will not eat over the next few days, but plan to take with you when you move.

Two Days Before the Move

Verify moving details and get ready to move.

❑ Contact the moving company to reconfirm logistics.

❑ Make sure the movers have directions to your old home and your new home.

❑ Get the name and phone number of the lead driver or mover.

❑ Get the name and phone number of the moving company manager or someone you can contact if there are problems during your move. Verify that this person will be available during the hours of your move.

❑ Provide the moving company with your phone number and contact information. If the movers are running late or have trouble finding your home, they should be able to contact you.

❑ Verify that you are properly insured and familiarize yourself with the policies and procedures for making insurance claims and damaged property claims.

❑ Familiarize yourself with the moving company's procedures now, as you may need to make a claim after your move.

❑ Make note of any deadlines. For example, how many days after the move do you have to file a claim?

❑ Will your home or renter's insurance company cover damages that are not covered by the moving company? Contact your insurance company to find out if you are insured during your move.

❑ Make payment arrangement plans.

❑ If you haven't already made payment arrangements, consider how you will pay the moving company.

❑ Will you use a credit card, check, or cash? If your employer is paying your moving costs, will your employer pay for moving costs directly, or will you be reimbursed?

❑ Will you tip the movers? Will you tip via cash, check, or electronic payment? Do you have enough cash on hand to tip the movers? If you are moving a long distance, ask if you will have the same movers at the beginning and end of your move. If not, consider providing separate tips for the movers who load your belongings at your old home and the ones who unload your belongings at your new home.

❑ Clean your home.

    ❑ Empty, clean, and defrost your refrigerator and freezer.

    ❑ Clean your oven, sink, and appliances.

    ❑ Clean your bathroom.

    ❑ Clean your bedroom, living room, and other living areas.

    ❑ Sweep, mop, dust, and vacuum.

    ❑ Keep your vacuum cleaner and broom handy, as you will need them the day of the move.

    ❑ Throw away trash.

❑ Optional: Make arrangements to have refreshments for the movers during the move. Refreshments are not required, but they are always appreciated. If you decide to provide refreshments, you do not have to spend a fortune on a fancy buffet. Although snacks and sandwiches are a big hit during a long, difficult move, something as simple as cold water on a hot day is genuinely welcomed and appreciated.

Moving Day

Meet the movers. Load your belongings. Conduct a move out inspection. Take inventory and move into your new home.

At Your Old Home

❑ Put snacks and refreshments in a convenient location (e.g., on the kitchen counter, in an empty room, in a cooler outside).

❑ If possible, place children and pets in the care of friends or family. If your children or pets will be on-site during the move, make sure they are in a safe place. Provide toys and activities to keep them entertained during the move.

- ❑ Pack your personal vehicle.
    - ❑ Transport valuable items, important documents, and sentimental items yourself.
    - ❑ If you have valuables that you do not want to leave in your home or vehicle during the move, consider getting a lock box or safe, temporarily leave the items with a trusted neighbor or friend, put the items in a safe deposit box, or hire a company that specializes in moving valuable items.
- ❑ Greet the movers. Give them a brief overview of your home's layout and provide moving instructions.
    - ❑ Know what you want done before the movers arrive. Do not bombard them with complicated moving instructions.
    - ❑ Let the movers know if there are items they should not move, how your boxes are grouped, and what should be loaded onto the truck last.
    - ❑ Clearly mark special items. If possible, put the items in a specific location. For example, put all of the suitcases in the same place and mark them with a sign that says "load last."
    - ❑ Make the movers' job as easy as possible. They will thank you and your move will go more smoothly.
- ❑ Supervise the movement of any valuable or fragile items. You cannot be everywhere during the move, but you should be nearby when your valuables are being loaded onto the truck. Try not to interrupt the movers' flow, but be available if they have questions or if you are needed to give specific instructions.
- ❑ If possible, after the movers clear a room, vacuum, sweep, and tidy up the space.
    - ❑ Let the movers know that you will be cleaning each room as soon as everything is moved out of it.

- ❑ I have done this while moving and it accomplishes two goals. One, I am out of the movers' way and they can continue making progress on the move without constantly bumping into me. Two, when they are done moving, I am done cleaning. I do not have to remain at the house after the move to continue cleaning.

- ❑ If you want to watch the movers load your items, ask friends or family members to clean the rooms as they are emptied. You can also assign someone else to watch the movers while you clean. If you prefer to hire professional cleaners, schedule a cleaning appointment for after the move.

- ❑ Remind the movers to load your vacuum cleaner, broom, and cleaning supplies onto the truck.

❑ Do a walkthrough.

- ❑ Ensure nothing has been left behind.

- ❑ Double check all rooms and spaces inside and outside your home.

- ❑ Check kitchen drawers, closets, cabinets, attic, basement, and garage.

❑ Have a move out inspection with your landlord or rental manager.

- ❑ Make sure your personal belongings are off the property.

- ❑ After the movers are done, give yourself at least 30 minutes to walk through the home, throw away trash and debris, and make sure the inside and outside of the property are clean and tidy.

- ❑ During the inspection, ask your landlord or rental manager if everything is as it should be. If there are damages, ask about costs and whether or not you will receive your entire deposit. If everything is fine, get confirmation in writing.

- ❑ If there is a move out checklist, go through it as you walk through the property. Make notes. Have your landlord or rental manager sign and date the checklist at the end of the inspection. If the landlord or rental manager wants to keep the checklist, ask for a copy of the checklist, or take a picture of it with your cell phone, and keep it with your moving documents.

- ❑ Inspection Tip: Take pictures of the condition of the property when you move out. I have had a landlord tell me the property was perfect when I moved out, only to receive a check for less than my full deposit. I used the pictures and move out checklist to get my full deposit. Keep all of your moving documentation. You never know when you'll need it.

❑ Lock up the home.

- ❑ Close windows and shades.
- ❑ Turn off lights.
- ❑ Lock doors, windows, and gates.

❑ Return your keys to your landlord or rental manager.

At Your New Home

❑ If you are renting, take pictures of your new home before you move in.

- ❑ Make note of any damages or needed repairs.
- ❑ Within a few days of moving in, contact your new landlord or rental manager to discuss any damages or necessary repairs. Check your lease to find out if there is a deadline for reporting pre-move in damages.
- ❑ When you move out later, you do not want to be responsible for paying for preexisting damage.
- ❑ Ideally, you want to take pictures before move in day.

However, if you cannot take pictures before the move, you may have to wait until your belongings have been moved in. If you delay the move to take pictures, the moving company may charge you for the extra time.

❑ Give the movers a brief overview of your home's layout and provide moving instructions.

❑ Let them know where to put your boxes. For example, point out the master bedroom, the children's rooms, and the office.

❑ If the movers will be placing items in a basement or attic, make sure the entryways to these spaces are kept clear throughout the move.

❑ Give your movers a copy of the scaled layout you made in week 7. Post a copy of the layout near the front door and keep a copy with you. You can also post a copy of the layout outside the door of each room.

❑ Provide the movers with directions regarding where to place large items (e.g., beds, couches, and tables). Ask them to put the items in their final, or near final, locations. You do not want to have to rearrange your furniture after the movers leave.

❑ Before the movers leave your new home, take inventory of your belongings and make sure everything has arrived.

❑ Double check your high value inventory form and make sure your items have arrived safely and undamaged.

❑ Check inside the moving truck to make sure nothing is left behind.

❑ Check for damaged items and crushed or opened boxes.

❑ Notify the lead mover or moving foreman of any damages.

❑ Make note of the damaged items so that you can file a claim.

❑ Take pictures of the damage for documentation.

❑ Tip the movers and thank them for their hard work. Thank your friends and family as well.

❑ Sign the bill of lading and keep a copy for your records.

Day After the Move

Welcome home! It is time to unpack.

❑ Begin by unpacking your essential items first. Locate your suitcases and unpack your open first box.

❑ Clean your home before you unpack everything. This may be the only time you get to see all those hidden nooks and crannies.

> ❑ If you cannot clean right after your move, consider hiring a cleaning service before you move in. You will receive a hefty discount by hiring a crew to clean an empty house.

> ❑ Ask your landlord, rental manager, or real estate agent if the home was professionally cleaned before you moved in. Depending on where you live, painting, carpet cleaning, and general maintenance may be required between tenants.

❑ Over the next few weeks, gradually unpack your nonessential items, reassemble furniture, and decorate your home.

❑ As you unpack, check for damaged items.

> ❑ If there are damages, check your moving agreement to verify the insurance claim and damage claim procedures.

> ❑ File your claim before the deadline.

> ❑ If necessary, contact the moving company manager to verify that your claim has been received and is being processed.

❑ Settle in and enjoy your new home.

Are there other items that you would like to include in your checklist? Add them to the *Let's Do This Checklist* – a blank checklist for your other "To Dos."

PEOPLE TO NOTIFY WHEN I MOVE CHECKLIST

The First to Know

- ❑ Family and Friends
- ❑ Employer/Human Resources
- ❑ United States Postal Service (USPS): https://moversguide.usps.com

Apps

- ❑ Coupons
- ❑ Maps
- ❑ News
- ❑ Weather

Children

- ❑ Babysitter
- ❑ Daycare
- ❑ Parent Teacher Association (PTA)
- ❑ Pediatrician
- ❑ Schools
- ❑ Scouts
- ❑ Youth Clubs/Organizations

Community

- ❑ Charities
- ❑ Civic Organizations
- ❑ Community Groups
- ❑ Library
- ❑ Neighborhood Associations

- ☐ Places of Worship
- ☐ Professional Associations
- ☐ Social Clubs

Education

- ☐ Alumni Associations
- ☐ Colleges/Schools
- ☐ Financial Aid
- ☐ Licensing/Certification Boards
- ☐ Registrar
- ☐ Student Loan Company

Finances

- ☐ Banks
- ☐ Car Loan Company
- ☐ Credit Card Companies
- ☐ Credit Reporting Agencies
- ☐ Credit Unions
- ☐ Home Equity Lender
- ☐ Loan/Finance Company
- ☐ Mortgage Lender
- ☐ Online Payment/Money Transfer Systems
- ☐ Retirement Accounts

Government Agencies

- ☐ Centers for Medicare and Medicaid Services (CMS)
- ☐ Citizenship and Immigration Services (CIS)
- ☐ Department of Motor Vehicles (DMV)
- ☐ Department of Veteran Affairs (VA)

- ☐ Internal Revenue Service (IRS)
- ☐ Federal Trade Commission (FTC)
  - ☐ National Do Not Mail/Do Not Call Registries
  - ☐ https://www.consumer.ftc.gov/articles/0262-stopping-unsolicited-mail-phone-calls-and-email
- ☐ Social Security Administration
- ☐ Voter Registration

Home Services

- ☐ Cleaning Service
- ☐ Home Security System
- ☐ Lawn Care
- ☐ Pest Control
- ☐ Pool Services
- ☐ Snow Removal

Insurance

- ☐ Auto Insurance
- ☐ Dental Insurance
- ☐ Disability Insurance
- ☐ Health Insurance
- ☐ Homeowner/Renter's Insurance
- ☐ Life Insurance
- ☐ Travel Insurance
- ☐ Vision Insurance

Medical

- ☐ Chiropractor
- ☐ Dentist
- ☐ Doctor/Primary Care Physician

- ❑ Gynecologist/Obstetrician
- ❑ Massage Therapist
- ❑ Optometrist/Optician
- ❑ Pharmacist

Memberships and Subscriptions

- ❑ Delivery Services
- ❑ Games
- ❑ Gyms/Health Clubs
- ❑ Movies
- ❑ Retail Clubs
- ❑ Subscription Boxes

Online

- ❑ Social Media Accounts
- ❑ Stores/Retailers
- ❑ Streaming Services

Periodicals

- ❑ Catalogs
- ❑ Journals
- ❑ Magazines
- ❑ Newspapers

Pets

- ❑ Kennel/Pet Boarding Services
- ❑ Pet Groomer
- ❑ Pet Insurance
- ❑ Pet Sitter
- ❑ Veterinarian

Professional Services

- ❑ Accountant
- ❑ Attorney/Lawyer
- ❑ Financial Advisor
- ❑ Investment Broker/Manager
- ❑ Tax Assessor

Transportation

- ❑ Airline Programs
- ❑ Car Rental Programs
- ❑ Emergency Road Service
- ❑ Travel Programs

Utilities

- ❑ Cable
- ❑ Electric/Power
- ❑ Gas
- ❑ Internet
- ❑ Telephone (Cell/Land Line)
- ❑ Satellite
- ❑ Sewage/Waste
- ❑ Trash
- ❑ Water

Miscellaneous

- ❑ _____
- ❑ _____
- ❑ _____
- ❑ _____

ORDER YOUR LIFE
APARTMENT AND HOUSE HUNTING CHECKLIST

Apartment/Community/Neighborhood Information

Name _____   Date Viewed _____

Address _____   Time Viewed _____

_____   Date Available _____

Landlord/Manager Contact Information

Name _____   Phone Number _____

Rent   Number of Bedrooms _____

$_____ Furnished   Number of Bathrooms _____

$_____ Unfurnished   Size/Square Feet _____

Length of Lease   **Commute Time**

❑   12 Months   Time to Work _____

❑   6 Months   Time to School _____

❑   Month-to-Month   Time to Public Transportation _____

❑   Other _____   Time to Food/Shopping _____

Deposits and Fees

❑   Security Deposit $_____   ❑   Pets Allowed

❑   Application Fee $_____   ❑   Pet Fee $_____

❑   First Month's Rent $_____   ❑   Parking Fee $_____

❑   Last Month's Rent $_____   ❑   Other $_____

Utilities   Included   Included

	Yes	No				Yes	No	
Cable	__	__	$_____	Internet	__	__	$_____
Electricity	__	__	$_____	Trash	__	__	$_____
Gas	__	__	$_____	Water	__	__	$_____
Heat	__	__	$_____	Other	__	__	$_____

Amenities

- ❑ Air Conditioning
- ❑ Alarm/Security System
- ❑ Balcony/Patio
- ❑ Business Center
- ❑ Clubhouse/Lounge
- ❑ Emergency Maintenance
- ❑ Fireplace
- ❑ Gym
- ❑ Playground
- ❑ Pool
- ❑ Storage $ _____
- ❑ Yard _____ sq ft

Parking

- ❑ Carport
- ❑ Garage
- ❑ Parking Lot
- ❑ Street
- ❑ None
- ❑ Other _____

Washer and Dryer

- ❑ Washer in Unit
- ❑ Dryer in Unit
- ❑ Hook-ups Only
- ❑ Nearby/On Site
  - $_____ Wash $_____ Dry
- ❑ None

Bedroom(s)

- ❑ Adequate Light in Room
  - ❑ Ceiling Lights
  - ❑ Natural Light
- ❑ Closet Space
- ❑ Cable Outlets
- ❑ Electrical Outlets
- ❑ Windows

Dimensions*   S M L

- (1) _____ sq ft __ __ __
- (2) _____ sq ft __ __ __
- (3) _____ sq ft __ __ __
- (4) _____ sq ft __ __ __

Bathroom(s)

- ❑ Shower and Bathtub
- ❑ Shower Only
- ❑ Bathtub Only
- ❑ Adequate Light in Room
  - ❑ Ceiling Lights
  - ❑ Natural Light
- ❑ Adequate Water Pressure
- ❑ Cabinet/Closet Space
- ❑ Electrical Outlets
- ❑ Windows

Dimensions*   S M L

- (1) _____ sq ft __ __ __
- (2) _____ sq ft __ __ __

Kitchen

- ❑ Adequate Water Pressure
- ❑ Adequate Light in Room
  - ❑ Ceiling Lights
  - ❑ Natural Light
- ❑ Cabinet Space
- ❑ Counter Space
- ❑ Dishwasher
- ❑ Electrical Outlets
- ❑ Garbage Disposal
- ❑ Microwave
- ❑ Oven/Stove __ Gas __ Electric
- ❑ Refrigerator
- ❑ Separate Dining Area
- ❑ Windows

Dimensions*   S M L

_____ sq ft __ __ __

Living Room

- ❏ Adequate Light in Room
  - ❏ Ceiling Lights
  - ❏ Natural Light
- ❏ Cable Outlets
- ❏ Electrical Outlets
- ❏ Windows

Dimensions*   S M L

_____ sq ft __ __ __

Floors and Windows

- ❏ Hardwood
- ❏ Carpet
- ❏ Tile
- ❏ Other Flooring _____
- ❏ Window Shades/Blinds

Safety

- ❏ Accessible Emergency Exits
- ❏ Alarm/Security System Works
- ❏ Carbon Monoxide Detector
- ❏ Doors Lock
- ❏ Lights Work
- ❏ Smoke Detectors Work
- ❏ Windows Lock
- ❏ Windows Open and Close

Neighborhood

__Urban __Suburban __Rural

- ❏ Feels Safe
- ❏ Good Schools
- ❏ Near Entertainment
- ❏ Near Food/Shopping
- ❏ Near Public Transportation
- ❏ Near School/Work
- ❏ Well-lit at Night

Notes _____

_____

_____

_____

*KEY: sq ft = square feet, S = small, M = medium, L = large

If you do not know a room's dimensions, describe the room as S, M, or L.

FORMS

ORDER YOUR LIFE HIGH VALUE INVENTORY FORM

Record information about your high value items on this form. Examples of high value items: antiques, artwork, china, collectibles, crystal, designer clothing, electronics, furs, jewelry, musical instruments, precious metals, rare documents, software, and tools.	

MOVING COMPANY			
ADDRESS			
PHONE NUMBER		EMAIL	
YOUR NAME			
ORIGIN/LOADING ADDRESS			
DESTINATION/ SHIPPING ADDRESS			

INVENTORY NUMBER	ITEM: DESCRIPTION AND NOTES	ESTIMATED VALUE

ADDITIONAL NOTES	
AT ORIGIN	
DATE	
AT DESTINATION	
DATE	

If your moving company has a high value inventory form, use the company's form.

ORDER YOUR LIFE MOVE IN/OUT INSPECTION FORM

TENANT NAME(S)	
ADDRESS	

MOVE IN DATE		INSPECTION DATE & TIME	
MOVE OUT DATE		INSPECTION DATE & TIME	

Record information about the condition of the property when you move in and when you move out. Take pictures and save them for your records.

This is a general move in/out inspection form. Use it as a guide. This form is not a substitute for legal advice, nor does it guarantee that your security deposit will be returned in full. Check your lease for move in and move out terms and conditions.

If your landlord or rental manager has a move in/out checklist, or a rental inspection form, use the form provided to you.

Use these abbreviations to rate the condition of the items listed below.
You can use more than one abbreviation per item (e.g., P, NRG).

E = Excellent **G** = Good **F** = Fair **P** = Poor	**NC** = Needs Cleaning **NP** = Needs Painting **NR** = Needs Repair **NRG** = Needs Replacing **NA** = Not Applicable

Inspected By	Move In	Move Out

	Move In	Move Out
Living Room	**Condition & Comments**	**Condition & Comments**
Ceiling		
Closet		
Doors		
Fireplace		
Floor/Carpet		
Light Fixtures		
Light Switches		
Lightbulbs		
Outlets		
Shades/Blinds		
Walls		
Windows/ Screens		
Additional Comments/ Other		

HALL/ENTRY	MOVE IN CONDITION & COMMENTS	MOVE OUT CONDITION & COMMENTS
Ceiling		
Closet		
Floor/Carpet		
Light Fixtures		
Light Switches		
Lightbulbs		
Outlets		
Additional Comments/ Other		

	MOVE IN	MOVE OUT
KITCHEN	CONDITION & COMMENTS	CONDITION & COMMENTS
Cabinets		
Ceiling		
Counters		
Dishwasher		
Doors		
Drawers		
Drip Pans		
Fan/Vent		
Faucet		
Floor		
Garbage Disposal		
Ice Maker		
Light Fixtures		
Lightbulbs		
Microwave		
Oven		
Oven Light		
Oven Racks		
Plumbing		
Refrigerator		
Refrigerator Light		
Sink		

KITCHEN	MOVE IN CONDITION & COMMENTS	MOVE OUT CONDITION & COMMENTS
Stove/Burners		
Walls		
Windows/ Screens		
Additional Comments/ Other		

	Move In	Move Out
BEDROOM 1	**CONDITION & COMMENTS**	**CONDITION & COMMENTS**
Ceiling		
Closet		
Doors		
Floor/Carpet		
Light Fixtures		
Light Switches		
Lightbulbs		
Outlets		
Shades/Blinds		
Walls		
Windows/ Screens		
Additional Comments/ Other		

BEDROOM 2	MOVE IN CONDITION & COMMENTS	MOVE OUT CONDITION & COMMENTS
Ceiling		
Closet		
Doors		
Floor/Carpet		
Light Fixtures		
Light Switches		
Lightbulbs		
Outlets		
Shades/Blinds		
Walls		
Windows/ Screens		
Additional Comments/ Other		

BATHROOM 1	MOVE IN CONDITION & COMMENTS	MOVE OUT CONDITION & COMMENTS
Bathtub		
Cabinets		
Ceiling		
Counter		
Doors		
Drawers		
Fan/Vent		
Faucet		
Floor		
Light Fixtures		
Light Switches		
Lightbulbs		
Mirror		
Outlets		
Plumbing		
Shelves		
Shower		
Sink		
Toilet		
Walls		
Windows/ Screens		
Additional Comments/ Other		

BATHROOM 2	MOVE IN CONDITION & COMMENTS	MOVE OUT CONDITION & COMMENTS
Bathtub		
Cabinets		
Ceiling		
Counter		
Doors		
Drawers		
Fan/Vent		
Faucet		
Floor		
Light Fixtures		
Light Switches		
Lightbulbs		
Mirror		
Outlets		
Plumbing		
Shelves		
Shower		
Sink		
Toilet		
Walls		
Windows/ Screens		
Additional Comments/ Other		

DINING ROOM	MOVE IN CONDITION & COMMENTS	MOVE OUT CONDITION & COMMENTS
Carpet		
Ceiling		
Doors		
Floor		
Light Fixtures		
Light Switches		
Outlets		
Shades/Blinds		
Walls		
Windows/ Screens		
Additional Comments/ Other		

OTHER	MOVE IN CONDITION & COMMENTS	MOVE OUT CONDITION & COMMENTS
Air Conditioning		
Carbon Monoxide Alarm		
Door Locks		
Dryer		
Fire Extinguisher		
Front/Back Porch		
Heating		
HVAC Filters		
Lawn/Garden		
Parking Area		
Patio/Deck		
Smoke Alarm		
Stairs		
Storage Room		
Thermostat		
Washer		
Water Heater		
Window Locks		
Additional Comments/ Other		

MOVE IN INSPECTION		
TENANT SIGNATURE(S)		DATE
		DATE
		DATE
LANDLORD/ AGENT/		DATE
RENTAL MANAGER SIGNATURE(S)		DATE

MOVE OUT INSPECTION		
TENANT SIGNATURE(S)		DATE
		DATE
		DATE
LANDLORD/ AGENT/		DATE
RENTAL MANAGER SIGNATURE(S)		DATE

MOVING BOX INVENTORY

Would you like to keep track of all of your belongings during your move? Use the Order Your Life Moving Box Inventory (https://orderyourlife.com/collections/digital-downloads/products/moving-box-inventory) to log your boxes and their contents. A good organizational system will save you countless hours, and considerable stress, when you start unpacking.

Watch my YouTube video *Moving Box Inventory: Excel How-To Series* (https://youtu.be/tmmRsRyY1M8) to learn more. Or read the transcript below. You can download the form as an Excel file or a PDF at OrderYourLife.com.

Transcript

>> TYWANQUILA: Hello, everyone. My name is Tywanquila Walker.

Welcome to the Order Your Life Excel How-To series. Today's topic is the Moving Box Inventory spreadsheet. During your move, use the Moving Box Inventory to keep track of your moving boxes and their contents.

00:24

In this video, I will cover how to enter room and content information. How to use dropdown menus. And how to add rows to the spreadsheet. First, let's take a look at the workbook.

00:44

This workbook has 2 tabs. An Instructions tab. And a Box Inventory tab. If you would like to read the instructions, you can find them on OrderYourLife.com. I have posted a link below in the description box.

01:03

The second tab is the Box Inventory tab. There are columns for box number, room, and contents. There are also columns to indicate whether each box's contents are fragile, have been loaded, have arrived at their destination, or were damaged during the move. Box numbers 1 through 100 have already been listed on this spreadsheet.

01:38

For the room, enter the name of the room where the box belongs. Use the dropdown menu to select the room name. If the room you want is not listed in the menu, type the name of the room.

02:00

For example, let's type Ray's Room. Under contents, write a description of what's in the box. Let's say that the box for Ray's Room has toy cars. Next, ask yourself, "Are the contents in this box fragile?" Use the dropdown menu to select yes or no.

Has the box been loaded? Yes or no? Did it arrive at its destination? Yes or no? And finally, was it damaged during your move? Yes or no?

02:56

Red, bolded text and symbols are used to draw your attention to boxes that may need special attention. For example, you should take pictures of damaged items and, if necessary, file an insurance claim.

03:16

If you need more than 100 rows, you can easily add rows to this spreadsheet. Let's scroll down to the bottom, and I'll show you how to do that. To add a row, type in any cell beneath the row. Here, let's type 101 and press enter.

03:38

You can type in any cell. For example, here let's type snow globes. And press enter.

03:48

You can also go to the last row and the last cell and press tab. And there you go. You have another row.

04:03

If you notice that the box number, room, or contents are not bolded, simply select those cells and click bold. And there you have it.

04:21

In this video, you have learned how to enter room and content information, use dropdown menus, and add rows to the spreadsheet.

04:34

If you have questions, email me at howto@orderyourlife.com. Thank you for watching the Order Your Life Excel How-to Series. Visit OrderYourLife.com for more exciting ways to get, and stay, organized.

TIPS

12 INGENIOUS PACKING TIPS

During your move, use twelve of my most ingenious packing tips.

1. Use hangers, trash bags, and rubber bands to pack your clothes. Your clothes will be easier to move and rehang in your closet. Plus, they won't get dirty during the move.

Method 1 – Use trash bags with drawstring ties. While your clothes are still on the hangers, pull a trash bag over your clothes and tie the drawstring closed around the base of the hanger hooks. For extra stability, crisscross the drawstrings before tying them or put a rubber band around the hanger hooks to keep them together.

Method 2 – Use trash bags without ties. While your clothes are still on the hangers, pull a trash bag over your clothes. Pull the bag to the base of the hanger hooks and put a rubber band around the hooks and the bag. This will close the bag and keep the hangers together. Alternatively, if you do not have rubber bands, tape the bag closed or use string to tie it closed.

2. Use towels and clothes instead of packing paper and bubble wrap. Instead of buying rolls of bubble wrap, use your towels, clothes, and scarves to protect fragile, breakable items. After you wrap and pack each item, give it a squeeze to make sure it is properly cushioned and protected.

3. Use your rolling suitcases. Pack heavy items, unwieldy items, or your clothes in rolling suitcases. If you pack heavy items, be mindful that you may have to lift the suitcase onto a moving truck, or carry it up a flight of stairs. Roll your belongings out of your old home and into your new home. Your back will thank you.

4. Put screws and bolts in labeled sandwich bags. Write the name of the piece of furniture on a sealable sandwich bag and put all of the screws, nuts, and bolts for that item in the bag. Seal the bag and either tape the bag to the furniture or put it in a specific box for all your screws and bolts. Use a separate bag for each piece of furniture. For desks and dressers, I tape the bags inside a drawer. For everything else, I put the bags in a labeled box (and make sure I know exactly where that box is at all times).

5. Put plastic wrap under bottle lids. Keep shampoo and other toiletries from spilling by unscrewing the lid, putting a layer of plastic wrap on top of the bottle, and screwing the lid back on. Make sure the lid is tight. This handy trick also works when you're traveling.

6. Keep your cutlery together with a plastic bag and tape. Instead of removing your forks and spoons from their holder and packing them separately, wrap the entire cutlery holder in a plastic bag. Seal the bag by putting a few loops of tape around the bag. When you reach your new home, simply remove the bag and tape and put your cutlery and holder in a kitchen drawer.

If you have a knife holder or cutlery block, this tip also comes in handy.

If you prefer not to use a plastic bag, use a towel, shirt, or other item of clothing to wrap your items.

7. Use masking tape to keep loose items together. Tape together loose cutlery, pens and pencils, and matching knickknacks. After I wrap my knives in a kitchen towel or potholder, I add a plastic bag and a few layers of tape to keep the knives secure and reduce the possibility of injury when I unpack. You can use the tape alone, without the plastic bag. However, the plastic bag keeps the tape from sticking to the items; it also makes removing the tape fast and easy.

8. Use comforter bags to pack linens and clothes. Pack your bed linens, towels, or seasonal clothes in comforter bags. If you are packing seasonal items, the comforter bags also serve as storage bags. When you arrive at your new home, simply put the storage bags in their permanent location – no unpacking necessary. I save my comforter bags when I buy new linens, then repurpose them for storing spare sheets and extra blankets. If you forgot to save your comforter bags, no worries. You can purchase storage bags for your move and repurpose them in your new home.

9. Use your trashcans as moving containers. Pack small kitchen appliances and utensils in your large trashcans. Pack bathroom accessories and toiletries in small trashcans. The goal is to put items from each room in their corresponding trash bins (e.g., kitchen items in kitchen trash bins). If the trashcan has a lid, tape the lid closed to prevent items from spilling out during the move. If the trashcan does not have a lid, put a trash bag in the can before packing your items, then seal the bag closed when the bin is full. Alternatively, after filling a small trash can, put the can in a larger box or bin; this keeps your items together in the bin but minimizes the chances that something will fall out during the move. Before using your trashcans for packing, give them a thorough cleaning; make sure they are suitable for use as moving containers. The last thing you want is to have to disinfect your trashcan and your belongings when you arrive at your new home.

10. Get free boxes. Get free boxes from local stores or friends who have recently moved. You can also search online. If you live near a Uhaul location, ask if they have any used, free boxes. Uhaul has a used box recycling program; customers return their boxes and other customers take the free boxes. Check with your Uhaul location often and early, as these free boxes can go quickly.

11. Label your boxes with color-coded moving labels. Use Order Your Life moving labels or moving kits (https://orderyourlife.com/collections/moving-labels) to easily organize your boxes and get them to the right room. Remember to put the labels on the sides of your boxes so you will be able to see the labels when the boxes are stacked on top of each other. Use the ribbon labels to help you identify the room label from the side or top of the box.

12. Use a moving guide or moving checklist. There are many things to do during a move, and it's difficult to remember everything.

I wrote the moving guide and checklist and I still have to refer to them when someone asks me about moving. Checklists will save you time and preserve your sanity. Checking each milestone off the list reduces stress and brings order to the chaos of moving. Make your list and check it twice.

I hope these tips work for you as well as they have worked for me.

NON-ALLOWABLES:
ITEMS NOT ALLOWED ON MOVING TRUCKS

Most moving companies will not transport hazardous or perishable items. These items are "non-allowables."

Below is a list of non-allowables. Use this list as a guide. For specific information, ask your moving company about items they will not transport.

Definitions

Hazardous – anything that is flammable, corrosive, or explosive (e.g., lighter fluid, gasoline, ammunition, batteries)

Perishable – anything that may spoil or die during transport (e.g., food, plants, living things)

Order Your Life List of Non-Allowables

Acetone	Charcoal
Acids	Chemicals
Adhesives	Chemistry Sets
Aerosols/Aerosol Cans	Cleaning Fluids/Solvents
Ammonia	Cologne
Ammunition	Combustible Liquids
Antifreeze	Cooking Oils/Fuels
Black Powder	Corrosive Liquids
Blasting Caps	Darkroom Chemicals
Bleach	Denatured Alcohol
Butane Tanks	Disinfectants
Camphor Oil	Dyes
Car Batteries	Dynamite

Engine Starting Fluids

Explosives

Fertilizers

Fire Extinguishers

Firearms

Fireworks

Flame Retardant Compounds

Flammable Goods

Flares

Food in Glass Jars

Frozen Foods

Fuels

Furniture Polish

Fuse Lighters

Gas/Gas Tanks

Gasoline

Hair Spray

Household Batteries

Household Cleaners

Igniters/Primers

Insecticides

Kerosene

Lacquer

Lamp Oil

Lighter Fluid

Lighters

Liquid Polishes

Liquor/Alcoholic Beverages

Loaded Guns

Matches

Motor Oil

Nail Polish

Nail Polish Remover

Oil Stains for Wood

Oils

Open/Partially Used Foods

Oxygen Tanks

Paint

Paint Remover

Paint Thinner

Perfumes

Pesticides

Petroleum Products

Pets

Plants

Poisons

Pool Chemicals

Produce

Propane

Propellants

Refrigerated Foods

Rubbing Alcohol

Rust Preventatives	Stains
Scuba Tanks	Starter Fuel
Shellac	Turpentine
Shoe Polish	Varnish
Smoke Devices	Weed Killer
Smokeless Powder	Yard Equipment Containing
Solvents	Fuel

High Value Items and Personal Possessions

In addition to hazardous and perishable items, ask your moving company if they transport valuable items and personal possessions (e.g., important documents, antiques, irreplaceable family photos). Even if your moving company will transport valuable, personal, sentimental, or sensitive items, consider moving these items yourself.

Here is a list of other items that may be non-allowables.

Antiques	Computer Hardware
Artwork	Computers/Laptops
Automobiles	Contraband
Birth Certificates	Credit Cards
Car Keys	Debit Cards
Car Titles	Deeds
Card Collections	Dental Records
Cash	Expensive Electronic Devices
Cell Phones	Family Heirlooms
Certificates of Deposit	Financial Documents
Checkbooks	House Keys
Coin Collections	Identification Cards

Insurance Documents	Safety Deposit Box Keys
Jewelry	School Records
Marriage Licenses	Social Security Cards
Medical Records	Stamp Collections
Medicine	Sterling Silver
Military Orders	Stocks/Bonds/Securities
Movie Collections	Tax Records
Moving Documents	Valuable Collections
Music Collections	Valuable Papers
Passports	Wedding Albums
Photo Albums	Wills
Photographs	Wine/Beer Collection
Professional/Work Files	

For more information about high value items and personal possessions, read *High Value Inventory*.

Record information about your high value items on the *Order Your Life High Value Inventory Form*.

TIPS FOR MOVING WITH CHILDREN

Here are tips for moving with children. Depending on your child's age, some tips will work better than others. Use whichever tips are most appropriate for your child and your situation.

- ❑ As soon as you know you are going to move, have a family meeting. Tell your children about the move. Let them know why you are moving.

- ❑ Use clear, simple explanations.

- ❑ Answer your children's questions and listen to their concerns.

- ❑ As you learn information about your new home, tell your children.

- ❑ Be honest. Don't exaggerate, oversell, or try to make things sound wonderful when they aren't. If you raise your children's expectations and don't deliver, they will be disappointed.

- ❑ Tell a story, read a book, or use playacting to explain the move.

- ❑ When you pack your children's belongings, explain that you aren't throwing their things away.

- ❑ Let your children help you pack.

- ❑ Let your children help you make decisions about what to keep and what to throw away.

- ❑ Let your children decorate their moving boxes.

- ❑ Use a special design or color for your children's moving boxes.

- ❑ Visit your new home with your children. Take a tour of the neighborhood.

- ❑ If you can't visit your new home, show your children pictures of their new home and school. Take them on a virtual tour.

- ❑ Help your children research their new home. Go online to learn about things you can do in your new community.

- ❑ Research schools and daycares near your new home.

- ❑ Help children say goodbye to their old home. Have a goodbye party, visit friends and family, or make a moving video, collage, or photo album.

- ❑ Help your children say hello to their new home. Get to know other families in the neighborhood, visit your children's school or daycare, or attend a community event.

- ❑ Take your children for health checkups (e.g., pediatrician and dentist) before you move.

- ❑ Get copies of your children's school records and medical history. You will need these documents to enroll your children in school.
    - ❑ School records
    - ❑ Report cards/transcripts
    - ❑ Standardized test scores
    - ❑ Birth certificates
    - ❑ Medical records

- ❑ Get information about your children's textbooks and class curricula. Take pictures of the textbook covers. The textbook pictures and course information will help school administrators place your children into the right class or grade at the new school.

- ❑ If your children are involved in special programs, get copies of test scores and program documentation.
    - ❑ Test scores (e.g., standardized, state, special programs)
    - ❑ Gifted program documents and program description
    - ❑ Individualized Education Plan (IEP)
    - ❑ Plans for classroom modifications

- ❑ Ask your healthcare provider to forward your children's medical records to your new healthcare provider.

- ❑ Throughout the move, keep your schedule for meals and bedtime the same. Routines are comfortable and familiar.

- ❑ During the move, let your children keep at least one comfort item (e.g., a toy, blanket, or book) nearby. Do not pack this item.

- ❑ Pack a "fun box" or "fun bag" to help your children get through the move. Include a few toys, books, or games for your children to keep them entertained. A "fun box" is great for travelling.

- ❑ If possible, arrange for your children to stay with a family member, friend, or babysitter on moving day.

- ❑ After the move, get your children's rooms in order first. It is comforting for children to be surrounded by familiar things.

- ❑ Be patient, understanding, and compassionate.

- ❑ Remember moving is stressful for adults and children.

For more information, read *Moving with Children*. Also check out *Moving Books for You and Your Child*.

MOVING BOOKS FOR YOU AND YOUR CHILD

You'll find links to the books below, and other moving books, on the Order Your Life Pinterest board called *Best Books About Moving and Moving On (https://tinyurl.com/movingbooks)*. The board is divided into multiple sections.

- ❑ Best Children's Book About Moving
- ❑ Best Moving Books for Adults
- ❑ Best Moving Books for Military Families
- ❑ Best Books About Moving On

Selection of Moving Books

- ❑ The Berenstain Bears' Moving Day by Stan Berenstain and Jan Berenstain
- ❑ Big Ernie's New Home: A Story for Young Children Who Are Moving by Teresa Martin and Whitney Martin
- ❑ Boomer's Big Day by Constance W. McGeorge
- ❑ Louis & Bobo: We Are Moving by Christiane Engel
- ❑ Moving House by Anne Civardi
- ❑ A House for Hermit Crab by Eric Carle
- ❑ The Leaving Morning by Angela Johnson
- ❑ A Kiss Goodbye by Audrey Penn
- ❑ Saying Good-Bye, Saying Hello...: When Your Family Is Moving by Michaelene Mundy
- ❑ Alexander, Who's Not (Do You Hear Me? I Mean It!) Going to Move by Judith Viorst
- ❑ My Very Exciting, Sorta Scary, Big Move: A Workbook for Children Moving to a New Home by Lori Attanasio Woodring

❑ Moving with Kids: 25 Ways to Ease Your Family's Transition to a New Home by Lori Collins Burgan

For more information, read *Moving with Children* and *Tips for Moving with Children*, and visit the Order Your Life Pinterest page.

TIPS FOR MOVING WITH PETS

The safety and comfort of your pet are important. Follow these tips to help your loved ones transition from their old home to their new home.

- ☐ Routines
    - ☐ Throughout the move, stick to your routines.
    - ☐ Feed your pet during regular feeding times.
    - ☐ Continue your pet's walk, play, and exercise schedule.
- ☐ Medical Checkup
    - ☐ Visit the veterinarian.
    - ☐ Make sure vaccines are up-to-date.
    - ☐ Get copies of your pet's vaccination record.
    - ☐ Refill your pet's prescriptions or get new prescriptions.
    - ☐ Get a health certificate. If you are moving out of state, you may need a veterinary-issued health certificate.
    - ☐ Talk to your veterinarian about your pet's anxiety. If the move will be stressful for your pet, ask your veterinarian about stress relieving medications.
    - ☐ Research veterinarians in your new neighborhood. Ask your current veterinarian for recommendations.
- ☐ Pet Sitter
    - ☐ Make arrangements for a friend, family member, or pet sitter to watch your pet on moving day.
    - ☐ Give the pet sitter detailed instructions for caring for your pet (e.g., time for feeding, walks, medication, and treats).
    - ☐ Provide food and toys for your pet.

- ❐ No Pet Sitter
  - ❐ Reduce your pet's stress by limiting exposure to noise and unfamiliar people. Keep your pet in a quiet place throughout the move.
  - ❐ If your pet will be in your home while you move, put your pet in a pet crate or quiet, empty room.
  - ❐ On the door of the room, post a sign that says "Do Not Enter. Pet Inside."
  - ❐ If possible, lock the door.
  - ❐ Tell the movers about your pet (e.g., type of pet, where the pet is located, and not to enter the room).
  - ❐ Provide food and toys for your pet.
- ❐ Pet Carrier
  - ❐ Get a pet carrier.
  - ❐ Inspect your pet carrier.
    - ❐ Make sure the carrier is in good condition,
    - ❐ Make sure the carrier locks properly.
    - ❐ Make sure the carrier is comfortable for your pet.
  - ❐ Place a towel or small blanket inside the carrier to keep your pet comfortable.
  - ❐ It may be comforting to your pet to have something in the carrier that smells like you. Consider putting items such as a t-shirt or pillowcase in the carrier.
  - ❐ Label the pet carrier. Include your pet's name, your name, and your contact information. If traveling by air, you may also need to include "Live Animal," "Fragile," "This Side Up," and "Keep at Room Temperature" labels. Ask your airline if special forms or labels are required.
  - ❐ A month before your move, help your pet get used to being

in the pet carrier. Begin by putting your pet in the carrier for a few minutes each day. Gradually increase the time until your pet is in the carrier for at least an hour every day. Let your pet sleep in the carrier. Talk to your veterinarian if your pet is having a hard time adjusting to being in the carrier.

- ❒ Travel Arrangements

  - ❒ Get an ID tag for your pet. The ID tag should include your pet's name as well as your name and contact information (e.g., cell phone number, new home address, and email).

  - ❒ Take a picture of your pet. If your pet gets lost, the picture will come in handy during your search.

  - ❒ Microchip your pet. If your pet gets lost, animal shelters and veterinary clinics can scan the chip.

  - ❒ Contact the microchip registry to register your name and phone number, or update your existing contact information if your pet already has a microchip.

  - ❒ If you are moving out of state, research the state's pet entry laws and regulations.

  - ❒ If you are moving out of the country, research quarantine times, vaccination requirements, and other legal requirements for pet entry. Depending on where you are going, your pet may be quarantined before entering the country.

  - ❒ Your pet may require special travel considerations during your move. Ask your veterinarian for advice on your pet's needs and your moving plans. Your veterinarian's advice is important, especially if you are traveling by airplane or in hot temperatures.

  - ❒ Ask your veterinarian how often and how much you should feed your pet during travel. The advice may be different for airline and car travel (e.g., a bumpy airline ride may make your pet nauseous).

- [ ] If traveling by airplane, contact the airline before booking your tickets. Ask about the travel policy for animals, fees, pet accommodations, pet travel documentation, weather and heat restrictions, and flight check in times. Ask about pet carrier requirements and Transportation Security Administration (TSA) regulations. Note that certain breeds of cats and dogs should not be transported by plane.
- [ ] If traveling by car, stop often for walks, play time, and restroom breaks.
- [ ] Research pet-friendly hotels. Contact the hotel before booking a room. Ask about pet fees, policies on pet type and size, and pet services.
- [ ] If your pet will not travel with you, research pet relocation services. There are companies that specialize in moving pets. Ask your veterinarian for recommendations.
- [ ] Pack Travel Essentials
  - [ ] Food
  - [ ] Water
  - [ ] Food and water bowls
  - [ ] Bedding
  - [ ] Grooming tools
  - [ ] Leash or harness
  - [ ] Litter box
  - [ ] Medications
  - [ ] Pee/potty pads
  - [ ] Towels or paper towels
  - [ ] Toys
  - [ ] Treats
  - [ ] Waste bags

- ☐ Waste scooper
- ☐ Your New Neighborhood
    - ☐ Find out if your new neighborhood has any ordinances, laws, or regulations pertaining to pets. Some communities limit the number of animals per household.
    - ☐ Search for pet friendly stores and recreation areas (e.g., pet supply stores and dog parks).
- ☐ After the Move
    - ☐ Set up your pet's bed and food bowl immediately. Familiar things will help your pet feel more at home.
    - ☐ Spend time with your pet. Reassure your pet that everything is okay.
    - ☐ Stick to your routines. Routines are familiar and comforting.
    - ☐ Until your pet becomes adjusted to your new home, keep your pet confined inside or near your home. Gradually give your pet more space to roam and explore. If you take your pet outside, use a leash so it doesn't wander off and get lost. It may take your pet several weeks to get used to its new home.
    - ☐ Interview potential veterinarians to see if they are a good fit for you and your pet.
    - ☐ Watch your pet for signs of stress or maladjustment. Talk to your veterinarian if you have concerns.

Pet Specifics

Are you wondering how to move your pet snake? What about your fish? Here are specific tips for different types of pets.

Dogs

- ☐ If traveling by car, take your dog on short trips to get it used to traveling.
- ☐ Consider putting your dog in a pet carrier. If a pet carrier is not

a good option for your dog, make sure your dog is comfortable during the drive and will not interfere with your driving.

- [ ] Before opening the car door, put a leash on your dog. After your dog is back inside the car and the door is closed, unleash your pet. Leashing your dog will prevent it from wandering away and getting lost.
- [ ] Clip your dog's nails to prevent scratches and damage to your car.
- [ ] Stop regularly for walks and exercise breaks.

Cats

- [ ] If traveling by car, take your cat on short trips to get it used to traveling.
- [ ] Put your cat in a pet carrier. The pet carrier will give your cat a comfortable, safe place to travel. Cats are independent creatures. They may try to return to your old home. The carrier will confine your cat so it doesn't get lost.
- [ ] Before opening the car door, put your cat in the pet carrier or attach a leash. After your cat is back inside the car and the door is closed, unleash your pet. Leashing your cat will prevent it from wandering away and getting lost.
- [ ] Clip your cat's claws to prevent scratches and damage to your car.
- [ ] Pack a litter box. During travel, give your cat access to the litter box.

Small Pets (e.g., hamsters, gerbils, rabbits)

- [ ] If traveling by airplane, get an airline approved pet carrier.
- [ ] If traveling by car, your small pet can usually travel in the cage it lives in.
- [ ] Make sure your pet's cage locks properly.
- [ ] To avoid spills, remove water and food containers from the cage.
- [ ] Place the cage in a secure, well ventilated area away from drafts.

Make sure the cage will not fall over.

- [ ] Protect your pet from cold drafts, direct sunlight, and extreme heat.

- [ ] Give your pet fresh water at every stop. Make sure it does not become dehydrated.

- [ ] Talk to your veterinarian about how often and how much you should feed your pet during travel.

Fish

- [ ] If traveling by airplane, contact an aquarium supply company or a pet supplier who specializes in fish. A knowledgeable representative can tell you how to pack your fish for air travel. For a fee, they may pack and ship the fish for you.

- [ ] If your fish are in a large aquarium, remove them from the aquarium and put them in smaller, unbreakable containers (e.g., a bucket with a lid or a leak-proof plastic bag).

   - [ ] Fish are sensitive to changes in water temperature. Use the water from the aquarium to fill the container.

   - [ ] Fill one-third to one-half of the container with water. Fish need air and water. Do not overfill the container with water.

   - [ ] Add your fish to the container. Do not overcrowd the fish. Depending on the fish species, each fish may need its own container.

- [ ] If possible, save 80% of the aquarium water and use it to refill the tank at your new home. Transport the water in large jugs or buckets with lids.

- [ ] Place the container in a secure area. Make sure it will not fall over during travel.

- [ ] For long distance moves, open the container a few times a day to refresh your fish's air supply.

- [ ] Talk to a veterinarian or pet supplier about how often and how much you should feed your fish during travel. Some fish species can survive days without food. If it is a short trip, you may not have to feed your fish.

- ☐ When you arrive at your new home, immediately set up your aquarium.
  - ☐ Set up equipment, filtration systems, and accessories.
  - ☐ Refill your aquarium with the saved water.
  - ☐ If you are adding new water, you may need to treat it. Buy water treatment at a pet supply store.
  - ☐ Run the filter for a few hours before returning your fish to the aquarium.
  - ☐ If your fish are in bags, let your fish adjust to the water temperature. Place the sealed bags in the aquarium. Let the bags float in the aquarium until the temperature between the bag water and aquarium water is the same. Once the temperatures are equal, pour the fish into the aquarium or use a net to transfer them.
  - ☐ If your fish are in buckets or other containers, make sure the container water and aquarium water are the same temperature. Pour the fish into the aquarium or use a net to transfer them.
  - ☐ Over the next few days, closely monitor your fish and the water conditions.
  - ☐ Give your fish time to adjust to their new surroundings.
- ☐ Ask a pet supplier about the best container for transporting your fish. Some fish can be safely transported in a leak-proof plastic bag. Other fish will need sturdier containers.

Birds

- ☐ If traveling by airplane, get an airline approved pet carrier.
- ☐ If traveling by car, your bird can travel in the cage it lives in.

- ☐ Make sure your bird's cage or carrier locks properly.

- ☐ During travel, cover your bird's cage. The covered cage will help keep your bird calm.

- ☐ To avoid spills, remove water and food containers from the cage.

- ☐ Place the cage in a secure, well ventilated area away from drafts. Make sure the cage will not fall over.

- ☐ Protect your bird from cold drafts, direct sunlight, and extreme heat.

- ☐ Give your bird fresh water at every stop. Make sure it does not become dehydrated.

- ☐ Talk to your veterinarian about how often and how much you should feed your bird during travel.

- ☐ After your move, put your bird in a place where it will not be disturbed. Give your bird time to become used to its new home.

Reptiles

- ☐ Reptiles can be transported in pet carriers, coolers, or other insulated containers. Ask your veterinarian about the best way to transport your pet.

- ☐ If traveling by airplane, get an airline approved pet carrier.

  - ☐ If your reptile is venomous, contact the airline and ask how your pet should be packed.

  - ☐ Ask about special labels or forms that have to be placed on the carrier.

  - ☐ Minimize possible disturbances to your pet. Tape a picture of your pet to the carrier. If your pet is unusual, the picture may reduce people's interest and curiosity during transport.

- ☐ If traveling by car, your reptile can travel in the cage or container it lives in.

  - ☐ If your pet lives in a large cage, consider getting a smaller, more secure cage or carrier.

- ☐ Make sure your pet is comfortable and has enough room to move around.
- ☐ Remove objects that could injure your pet during the move.
- ☐ For a large reptile, consider transporting your pet in a cloth reptile bag.
- ☐ For a small reptile, consider transporting your pet in a deli cup. Make sure there are ventilation holes in the lid.
- ☐ If your pet needs a wet environment, place moist towels in the carrier to prevent dehydration. Pack a water bottle and mist your pet as needed.
- ☐ Place the carrier in a secure, well ventilated area. Make sure the carrier will not fall over.
- ☐ While traveling, keep your pet at a comfortable temperature.
  - ☐ If necessary, use heat packs or cold packs.
  - ☐ Do not place the packs directly next to your reptile (e.g., tape the packs to the top of the carrier or loosely wrap the packs in a towel or newspaper before placing them in the carrier).
  - ☐ Use a temperature gun or gauge to monitor temperature.
- ☐ After your move, put your pet in a place where it will not be disturbed. Give your reptile time to become used to its new home.
- ☐ Talk to your veterinarian about how often and how much you should feed your pet during travel.

Horses

- ☐ If you will be towing your horse in a horse trailer, plan overnight stops in advance.
  - ☐ Research stable options along your route.
  - ☐ Contact hotels to ask if your horse and horse trailer can be

parked in the parking area overnight.

- ☐ If you are camping, ask if horses are permitted on the campgrounds.

☐ Train your horse to enter and exit the trailer. Practice safely loading and unloading your horse. Make sure you and your horse are comfortable with the process.

☐ If you have never loaded a horse trailer before, ask a horse trainer or trained professional for help.

☐ If you are not familiar with horse trailers, ask your veterinarian or a horse trainer which type of horse trailer would be best for your horse.

☐ Practice driving with the trailer before traveling a long distance with your pet.

☐ Research your new neighborhood's laws for pasture size and minimum distance from the barn to your house.

☐ Research stables and stabling options in your new neighborhood.

☐ Talk to your veterinarian about how often and how much you should feed your pet during travel.

3 TIPS TO LOWER YOUR TAXES AND SAVE MONEY ON YOUR MOVE

Did you know you can deduct your moving expenses on your tax return?

To be eligible for a moving expenses deduction, your move must be related to work. Did you start a new job, transfer to a new location, or move for other work-related reasons? If so, you may qualify for a deduction.

Here are three important tips to help you lower your tax burden.

1. Have Eligible Moving Costs

Answer the following questions to find out if you have eligible moving costs.

Q1: Did you move to a tropical island, buy your dream home, or move to the big city? Congratulations! You're living a grand and wonderful life. Do you qualify for a moving deduction? That depends, see Q2.

Q2: Did you move because of work? Yes? Well, you're in luck. To be eligible for a moving deduction, you must be moving because of work.

Q3: Do you pass the time test? To pass the time test, within the first 12 months after your move, you must start your new job and work full-time for at least 39 weeks.

Q4: Do you pass the distance test? To pass the distance test, find the distance from your old home to your new job. Then, find the distance from your old home to your old job. If the distance from your old home to your new job is at least 50 miles more than the distance from your old home to your old job, you pass the distance test.

Sounds odd, right? Let's walk through an example. Let's say the distance from your old home to your new job is 60 miles, and the distance from your old home to your old job was 3 miles. Because 60-3

= 57 miles, you pass the distance test.

In contrast, let's say the distance to your new job is 60 miles, and the distance to your old job was 11 miles. You do not pass the distance test because 60-11 = 49 miles.

If you are a member of the Armed Forces and your move is due to a military order and permanent change of station, you do not have to satisfy the time test or distance test.

Q5: Did you pay your moving expenses? You can only deduct moving expenses that you yourself have paid. If your employer paid some of your moving costs, or you will be reimbursed, you cannot deduct those expenses.

Now that you know you're eligible for a tax deduction, which moving expenses can you deduct?

2. Deduct Every Moving Expense You Can Imagine

You can, and should, deduct the cost of hiring movers to transport your goods from point A to point B. However, I bet there are at least three other moving expenses you can deduct. Any expense that is both reasonable and necessary for your move counts as an eligible deduction. How many of these moving expenses can you claim?

❑ Cost of connecting or disconnecting utilities

❑ Cost of shipping your vehicle

❑ Cost of shipping your pets

❑ Cost of rental trucks

❑ Cost of moving pods

❑ Cost of hiring movers

❑ Cost of hiring packers

❑ Cost of moving help (e.g., hiring a professional organizer to help you move)

❑ Cost of transporting or moving your household goods

- ☐ Cost of moving your household goods from a place other than your former home (Yes, you can deduct the cost of moving your things from storage, your grandma's house, or your cousin's garage.)
- ☐ Cost of storing and insuring household goods
- ☐ Storage fees
- ☐ Gas or mileage on your vehicle
- ☐ Cost of staying at a hotel (if you are moving a long distance)
- ☐ Parking fees
- ☐ Tolls
- ☐ Cost of moving boxes
- ☐ Cost of moving supplies (yes, packing tape counts)
- ☐ Order Your Life Moving Kit (https://orderyourlife.com/collections/moving-labels; Yes, this is a tax-deductible expense.)

3. Use the IRS Interactive Tax Assistant

You know the IRS has a million rules about what you can and cannot deduct from your taxes. Lucky for us, there is the Interactive Tax Assistant (ITA) tool. Specifically, the ITA tool called Can I Deduct My Moving Expenses? (https://www.irs.gov/help/ita/can-i-deduct-my-moving-expenses) will guide you through a list of questions to help you determine your eligibility to deduct moving expenses. In less than 10 minutes, you will know whether you qualify and which expenses you can deduct.

Want to know more? Go to the IRS website to learn more about moving expenses and the many tools available through the Interactive Tax Assistant (https://www.irs.gov/help/ita).

Note: Due to tax reform under the Tax Cuts and Jobs Act (TCJA), tax deductions for moving expenses have been suspended until 2025.

4 TIPS TO UNPACK LIKE A PRO

Now that you have moved into your new home, you are probably wondering what to do next.

What should I unpack first? How do I navigate through all of the boxes in my home? How do I turn chaos into order?

Follow these unpacking tips and you will be well on your way to settling comfortably into your new abode. Think of this as a starter guide to your unpacking expedition.

1. Start with the End in Mind

After a long day of moving, you are probably exhausted and ready for a nice long nap. Good! This feeling will remind you to start with the end in mind – sleep. The end encompasses your need to sleep and relax at the end of a long, hard day.

Begin your unpacking adventure by setting up your bed, your children's beds, and your pets' beds. If you live with extended family or friends, help them set up their beds too.

Providing everyone with a comfortable place to sleep will make your place feel more like home. In addition, knowing where you're going to lay your head at the end of the day will relieve some of your stress.

Don't worry about setting up the entire bedroom. Focus on the sleeping area and clean linens. Focus on having your child's favorite stuffed animal ready for a bedtime cuddle. Focus on your dog, cat, or bird settling down for the night. Focus on that small nest or haven where you will finally get to lay your head and drift off into dreamland.

You don't need to have everything in place to enjoy a good night's sleep. Attend to the basics of setting up a good, cozy sleep area and you will have successfully achieved the art of step 1 – starting with the end in mind.

2. Focus on the Staples and Feed Your Hunger

Now that you have a place to sleep, it is time to focus on your kitchen. Similar to preparing your sleeping area, don't try to unpack everything at once. Simply unpack what you need and place items in their permanent (or near-permanent) locations.

Gather the staples you need to feed your family and keep your energy flowing.

Even if you don't plan to cook a grand meal the first night (or the first week) after moving in, unpack the kitchen basics (e.g., plates, cups, pots, pans, utensils, coffee maker, tea kettle, microwave). At the very least, have disposable dishware, utensils, and napkins on hand for when you order take out, make breakfast, or have a snack.

On your first grocery shopping trip, purchase the staples (e.g., coffee, cereal, eggs, fruit, vegetables, pasta, canned goods, frozen foods). If you have the option, skip the line at the store and use a grocery delivery service, shop online and pick up in store, or have your groceries delivered via mail.

No matter your shopping method, purchase enough food for a few days to a week. Order enough to get you through the early transition phase of moving into a new home.

Adjust the lists of previously mentioned kitchen basics and staples to fit your and your family's needs. Think about what you use and eat often. Let that be your guide to deciding what to unpack and purchase first. Focus on the foods you and your family enjoy, but are easy to prepare.

When you want to have a drink of water, eat a bowl of cereal, or enjoy your morning cup of tea, all you'll have to do is reach in the kitchen cupboard to get what you need. Having basic dishware and easily preparable foods at your fingertips will save you hours of frustration searching for the things you need.

At the end of the first or second week of your new home, when everything is relatively settled and your family is starting to establish a new routine, make a grand meal to celebrate moving in. Incorporate some of your favorite dishes and comfort foods to make you truly feel at home.

3. Prepare to Entertain (Yourself)

Are you wondering what to do when you need a break from unpacking? Are you searching for ways to keep your children and other family members entertained? Yes?

It's time for step 3 – prepare to entertain yourself and your loved ones.

The easiest entertainment options include your phone, tablet, computer, handheld video game console, art supplies, puzzles, puzzle books, or your child's favorite toy. All of these options are easy to set up and require little time or energy.

On the other hand, if you want to experience the full entertainment experience and give yourself a space to relax in the mist of moving and unpacking, consider setting up your full entertainment system, including comfy furniture.

Assemble and organize your entertainment center, television, video games, and sound system. Place your couch in the perfect location. Pull up your coffee table and favorite chair and settle in for a temporary distraction.

As mentioned previously, you don't have to get everything perfectly settled. A relatively organized space with comfortable places to sit will go a long way towards making your new home feel more livable. As an added bonus, you'll know exactly where to find your family members as you unpack.

Clear out a space for rest breaks and friendly entertainment. You may even be able to unpack a box or two while you watch your favorite show.

4. Embrace a Clean Slate

One frustrating thing about moving is all the boxes, paper, and crates you have to put away after you unpack. To minimize your frustration, practice embracing a clean slate.

As you unpack, put items in their new homes (i.e., their permanent locations). Refrain from unpacking items and letting them sit around homeless, taking up precious counter and floor space. Focus on one room at a time and put things in their proper places.

Immediately take out your trash and recyclables.

After you unpack a cardboard box, break it down (i.e., remove the tape and lay it flat) and prepare it for recycling or the trash bin. If recycling is an option, put packing paper in a designated recycling bin. Put trash in trash bags. Place everything by the front door and, during the course of your unpacking expedition, take these unwanted items out of your new home as soon as you can and as often as you can.

Think of your trips to the trash bin as a break from unpacking. Give yourself a moment to enjoy a sense of accomplishment.

Constantly clean as you go, and make a clean sweep of your home at the end of each day.

Embrace a clean slate and you will reap the joys of having a tidy house as you unpack like a moving pro.

5 CLEVER AND CREATIVE WAYS TO ORGANIZE YOUR STUFF

The best way to stay organized is to have less stuff.

However, if you don't know what to throw away, can't part with your belongings, or you just aren't ready to start simplifying and minimizing your life, begin by organizing what you have.

As you organize your stuff, think about what you need, what you use often, and what you may be able to let go. When you can proudly show off all the things you love, do you really need that other stuff?

Seriously ponder that question as you declutter and organize your life.

Clever and Creative Solutions to Organization

Here are five creative ways to organize the things you love.

1. Keep It Together

Put similar items in the same location or in the same container. Clear containers make the perfect holding stations for toy cars, stationary, school supplies, eating utensils, snacks, and tiny knickknacks that go missing when they are not contained.

2. Track It Up

Take advantage of unused wall space. Use a track system, or pegboard, to vertically store brooms, tools, sports equipment, purses, hats, jewelry, scarves, and ties. In addition to getting items off the floor, this vertical storage system allows you to see everything at a glance.

3. Bag It

Give the back of a door a new purpose. A hanging shoe organizer is the perfect way to organize your shoes. It's also a perfect way to store cleaning supplies, towels, personal hygiene items, stuffed animals, art supplies, pantry items, and your favorite snacks.

4. Store It

Keep rarely used items out of sight until you need them. Use a beautiful bench as furniture and for storage. Store blankets, pillows, towels, toys, board games, or winter gear in a storage bench. The bench serves as extra seating and as a hideaway for items you don't use every day.

5. Float Above It

Turn a boring wall into a work of art, and a great display case. Floating shelves add a bit of flair to an otherwise nondescript room. Use floating shelves to store your books, nail polish, paintings, trophies, coin collection, toiletries, or children's artwork.

Get creative, and get organized. Look around your home and office. Where can you use these five clever tricks to add flair and order to your life?

7 TIPS TO ORGANIZE YOUR LIVING ROOM

Are your ready to turn your living room into a showroom? Or, at the very least, do you want to create a clutter-free space of which you can be proud?

Read my seven tips to get your living room in tiptop shape. The steps are easy to follow. Plus, you only need 10 minutes a day.

7 Steps and 10 Minutes to a Clutter-free Space

1. Use a Timer

Set aside 10 minutes a day to clean and organize your living room. Set your timer for exactly 10 minutes. When the timer goes off, stop. You're done. You can begin again tomorrow.

2. Get Everyone Involved

Turn your 10-minute cleanup into a family gathering. Get everyone involved. Make it a party by adding music.

Let all who dwell in your home join in the fun. Let's be honest, you probably didn't make a mess all by yourself. It's only fair that you share the joy of cleaning.

Young children can put away their toys while older children sweep or vacuum. Give everyone a job that can be done in 10 minutes or less. Stay upbeat and everyone will feel accomplished when the timer goes off.

3. Go Silent

Turn off the television and put away all electronic devices. If you are using the timer on your device, put your device in do not disturb or airplane mode.

With the exception of some good music, go silent. Focus all of your attention on the task at hand.

After you've organized for 10 minutes, feel free to pick up your phone and post pictures of your accomplishments.

4. Divide and Conquer

Divide big tasks into smaller tasks. Pace yourself. Do a little every day.

How long did it take your living room to get in the state it's in? Did it take more than 10 minutes? Probably.

It's unlikely you'll get everything done in 10 minutes. No worries. Congratulate yourself for 10 minutes of hard work. High five! You'll be back tomorrow.

5. End the Day with a Win

Clean and organize your living room at the end of the day. Do you relax in your living room before going to bed? Give it a quick cleaning before heading off to dream land.

Go to bed feeling like a winner. You set a goal and you accomplished it. Congratulations!

6. Love What You See

Only display the things you love. Put the I-might-need-this-laters and the so-in-so-gave-me-this-so-I-have-to-keep-it-out-even-if-I-don't-want-tos somewhere else.

Consider donating items you don't love. Give them away to a friend who really wants them or needs them. If you can't part with an item now, store it away for six months. If you still don't love it in six months (or you haven't used it), get rid of it.

Every item deserves a good home. Only keep the items you love.

7. Keep It Simple

Keep your cleaning and organizing routine simple. Complete small tasks. Stop when the timer stops. Congratulate everyone for their efforts.

If you clean your living room for 10 minutes every day, you will complete 1 hour and 10 minutes of effortless cleaning each week. That's 3650 minutes a year, or 60 hours and 50 minutes. Not bad for 10 minutes a day! Well done!

HOW TO ORGANIZE YOUR CLOSET IN 10 EASY STEPS

Is your closet bursting at the seams? Does finding clothes or getting dressed result in wasted time and unnecessary stress? A cluttered, disorganized closet can turn a simple task into a herculean effort. But it doesn't have to be that way.

In 10 easy steps, transform your cluttered closet into an organized haven. Save time and energy while maximizing your closet space. I'll show you how to effectively organize your closet, one step at a time.

Step 1: Assess

Before diving into organizing, assess your current closet situation. Is your closet overflowing? Do you have items in your closet that belong somewhere else? Is everything jumbled, which makes it difficult to find items when you need them?

Write down your main closet dilemma. Then write down your primary closet organization goal. Post your dilemma and your goal where you can see them (e.g., on your closet door, on your bedroom wall, on your dresser mirror). Keep your goal (and dilemma) in mind throughout your organizing journey.

Step 2: Prepare

Prepare your workspace. Clear a space where you can sort through the items in your closet. This may be a corner of the room, a corner of the closet, a table, desk, or dresser, or a small space on your bed. This space is your designated work area.

If you have a tendency for your workspace to expand and spread into areas where it shouldn't, set boundaries around your work area. For example, mark off your workspace with colorful removable tape or ribbons.

If you don't have a lot of room to maneuver, or your workspace is small, work in small batches. Remove a few items from your closet at a time, then categorize and sort them as discussed in steps 3 and 4.

Step 3: Categorize

Divide your workspace into three areas: Keep, Donate, and Discard. Label the three areas. Keep your areas separated.

To make sure you don't accidentally throw away something you plan to keep, label your bins, bags, or boxes. You can also use different colored tape, markers, bags, or bins to distinguish your keep, donate, and discard piles.

Remove each item from your closet. Decide if you will keep, donate, or discard it. Put the item in the appropriate area of your workspace.

Step 4: Sort and Toss

As you sort through your belongings, be honest with yourself. Examine each item and ask yourself, "Does this item fit me? Do I need it? Will it better serve someone else? Is it damaged beyond repair?" Donate or discard anything you no longer wear or no longer need.

Keep: To streamline your organizing efforts, group similar items together (e.g., shirts, pants, dresses, jackets). Within each category, further sort items by color or style. Sorting your items now will make it easier to place similar items together when you put everything back in your closet. It will also make it easier for you to find what you need.

Donate and Discard: Remove these items from your workspace as soon as possible. After you fill a donation box, seal the box and place it near your front door, put it in your car, or immediately take it to a donation center. After you fill a discard bag, put it near your front door or immediately take it outside and put it in the trash bin.

Don't let your workspace become crowded with items you have already sorted.

Step 5: Fold and Hang

Keep: If you have the space, go ahead and fold your keep items or put them on hangers. If your space is limited, you may have to temporarily put your items in bins or boxes until you can return them to your closet. Place your neatly folded items in your bins. Label the bins by clothing type, color, or style.

Donate: You don't have to sort your donations by color or style, but you should fold the items. Folding maximizes space in your bins and it may make the donation center representative's job easier.

Step 6: Consider Containers

To make the most out of your closet space, consider using clear storage containers, baskets, bins, shoe racks, or hanging organizers. There are many creative ways to organize your belongings.

In addition to maximizing your storage space, clear containers are a good solution for storing out-of-season items, small oddly shaped items, or items that may fall off their hangers or end up on the floor. If you use containers, measure the space inside your closet to make sure the containers will fit.

Step 7: Focus on Function

When your closet is empty, take a look inside and focus on function. Decide where you want each item to go. Draw a sketch of your closet and label the sketch with the future locations of your belongings. Include the locations and dimensions of storage containers in your drawing.

Place the type and style of clothes you wear often near the front of the closet. Place anything you rarely wear or use near the back of the closet or on an out-of-the-way shelf.

Group clothes and shoes by type or function (e.g., athletic, work, formal wear). Group items that are reserved for special occasions. Group items that you really want to throw away, but don't have the heart to discard yet.

Step 8: Stare and Compare

Compare the keep items in your workspace to your carefully labeled closet sketch. Will the items you plan to keep fit in your closet?

If no, reassess and resort your keep pile. Can you donate or discard additional items? Are there items in your keep pile that do not belong in the closet?

Not every item needs to be hung, nor does it have to be stored in your closet. Consider finding alternative locations for your additional keep items. For example, fold them instead of hanging them. Place them in storage containers. Place them in a dresser drawer.

Now that you've stared, compared, and reassessed, will everything fit in your closet? If yes, you are ready for step 9.

Step 9: Reassemble

You have a plan sketched out, and it is time to put things back in your closet. As you reassemble your closet, refer to your diagram.

Group items by type and function. To make wardrobe and outfit selection easier, further group items by color. Arranging your items by color has two benefits – it makes things easier to find and it creates a colorful, appealing space.

Hang clothes that wrinkle easily. If possible, use hangers or organizers that are appropriate for each type of item (e.g., non-slip hanger, pant hanger, notched hanger, tie rack, purse hanger, handbag organizer, shoe rack).

Place neatly folded items on shelves, in drawers, or in storage containers. Folding items maximizes space.

After you reassemble your closet, check your workspace to make sure you didn't miss any items. Is everything accounted for and back in the closet? Good. Tidy up your workspace and give yourself a round of applause.

Congratulations! Take a step back and admire your neatly arranged closet. Send pictures to your family and friends.

Step 10: Maintain

No organizing effort is complete without this last important step – maintain good order. Make a habit of maintaining your organized closet.

Frequently donate or discard anything that no longer serves you. Return misplaced items to their designated spaces. Fold or hang untidy items. Establish a system for managing dirty laundry (e.g., use a hamper or laundry bag; set up a designated area in your laundry room).

Set aside a few minutes each month, or half an hour every three months, to assess your closet space. If you update your wardrobe frequently, set aside more time or conduct maintenance more regularly. Set a maintenance schedule that works for you and your lifestyle. Keep your closet neat and clutter-free with regular maintenance.

Organizing your closet doesn't have to be a daunting task. With a systematic approach, dedication, and ten easy steps, you can transform your closet into an organized, functional space.

Assess. Categorize. Sort. Maintain. Repeat.

Strive to create a harmonious space with less clutter, less stress, and more room to breathe.

HOW TO ORGANIZE ANYTHING

At first glance, organizing seems like a daunting task. However, with the right mindset, you can organize anything. My how to organize anything exercise is outlined below.

For easy, straightforward problems, I go through this process in my head. In contrast, when problems are challenging, I write out the steps I need to take to organize my life.

Writing things down helps me formalize next steps and actions. It is also an informal written contract that I make with myself and use as a guidepost to achieve my goals. I'm sharing my process with you because it might help you, too.

How to organize anything is designed to take 10 to 20 minutes, get you in the frame of mind to organize, and familiarize you with implementing and reiterating solutions.

The how to organize anything exercise can be used to tackle any situation that requires organizing and planning. The technique can also be used in everyday situations when you are finding it difficult to come up with solutions to your problems.

The beauty of how to organize anything is that it forces you to get to the root of the problem and quickly begin implementing solutions.

The hardest step to organizing anything is getting started. Use this exercise to put your thoughts into action. Take the next step on the path to ordering your life.

How to Organize Anything

1. Define the What

Determine what you want to do. Find your what by asking yourself a few questions.

What am I trying to do? What do I want to accomplish? What is my end goal? In a few words, clearly state your what.

2. Ask Why

Ask yourself why multiple times.

Ask yourself why. Then ask yourself why again. Why am I doing this? Why do I need to do this? Why do I need to stop doing this?

Each successive why question should be a follow-up to the previous why question. There should be a logical flow of whys that lead from one question to the next.

Ask yourself why until you get to the root of the problem. Usually, you will ask why 3 to 5 times. If you find yourself asking why 10 times, you have gone too far. You have either misinterpreted the root cause of the problem, misunderstood the root cause, or started tackling an entirely new problem.

Let's look at some examples.

Everyday Example

Question: Why am I so tired today? Answer: I didn't sleep well last night.

Question: Why didn't I sleep well last night? Answer: The baby kept crying.

Question: Why was the baby crying? Answer: She's sick and doesn't feel well.

Organizing Example

Question: Why won't all of my clothes fit in my closet? Answer: I don't have enough space.

Question: Why don't I have enough space? Answer: I bought 10 new outfits for my new job.

Question: Why did I buy new outfits? Answer: The old ones don't suit me anymore.

Question: Why don't the old ones suit me anymore? Answer: They are out of fashion.

Question: Why am I hanging on to old clothes that are out of fashion? Answer: Insert your own answer here. If your answer still focuses on your clothes and your closet, you are ready to think about solutions. If your answer focuses on how your mother gave you those clothes and you can never throw away anything she gave you, you have stumbled onto a new problem. Stumbling onto a new problem is fine, as long as you make a commitment to address that problem (and the original problem with which you started).

Your answer to the last why question will help you brainstorm solutions. What are you going to do next?

3. Brainstorm Solutions

Brainstorm possible solutions and write down everything that comes to mind. When you can't think of any more solutions, move on to step 4, weighing the pros and cons.

If you are the type of person who can spend hours brainstorming, put a time limit on how long you will spend brainstorming or limit how many solutions you will generate. For example, limit your brainstorming session to 3 minutes, or say you will stop when you get to 8 solutions.

How to organize anything is designed to be a quick process. If you need more time, you can always reiterate, as you will see in step 8.

4. Weigh Pros and Cons of Solutions

Now that you have a list of options, write down the pros and cons of each solution. Focus on the major pros and cons and try not to get down into the minutiae of each option. The list should not be exhaustive. Hit the high points and move on.

5. Rank Solutions

As you wrote your pros and cons, you likely gained some insights into which solutions would work best for your situation. Rank your solutions based on their feasibility, achievability, and time constraints.

Description of Terms

- Feasibility – how easy it is for you to implement the solution
- Achievability – how likely you are to accomplish your goal using the solution
- Time constraints – how likely you are to accomplish your goal given the amount of time you have to implement the solution

After you rank your possible solutions, focus on the solutions that are most feasible and achievable in the time you have.

6. Evaluate Top Solutions

Evaluate your top ranked solutions. Only look at your top 2 or 3 solutions, as these are likely the solutions you will implement. Write a short description of the benefits of each solution.

What value is the solution? What are the long term benefits? What are the short term benefits?

7. Focus and Implement One Solution at a Time

Get to work and begin implementing your solutions. Find out what works by focusing on one solution at a time.

If you implement multiple solutions simultaneously, you may miss something or overlook a long-term solution that really works. Oversights are possible when you try to do too many things at once.

Granted, sometimes it makes sense to implement two solutions at the same time (e.g., sorting clothes into donate and keep piles while simultaneously sorting the keep pile by clothing type). That said, if you decide to implement two solutions at once, make sure the processes are complimentary and do not interfere with each other.

If the processes interfere, implement one solution in its entirety. Then, move on and implement the next solution.

8. Iterate and Reiterate

Iterate and reiterate each solution until you achieve your desired results. You may have to implement a solution more than once, or incorporate a solution that did not rank among your top 3 solutions but fits your needs. As long as you keep your end goal in mind, refining your solution is normal and acceptable.

If necessary, repeat the entire how to organize anything process. Redefine your what. Reassess your whys. Reinvigorate yourself to achieve your goals.

Organizing is an iterative process. It takes time to find the right solution.

9. Keep Time in Mind

Dedicate 10 to 20 minutes to this how to organize anything exercise. Remember, this is a guide to get you moving in the right direction. It gets you started on the process of organizing. It is not designed to take 8 hours.

If you find yourself spending more than 20 minutes on your first iteration of completing this exercise, you are overthinking things. You can always come back later and do the exercise again (i.e., reiterate).

The goal is to make a plan and take action. Do a quick analysis of the problem, evaluate your solutions, and get to work.

Example: All the Steps

Here is an example of all the steps in action.

1. Define the What

- Organize my email inbox

2. Ask Why

- Why do I need to organize my email inbox?
  ○ I get too many emails.
- Why do I get too many emails?
  ○ I'm signed up for a lot of newsletters that I don't read.
- Why am I signed up for a lot newsletters?
  ○ I wanted the coupons.

- Why am I not reading the newsletters?
  - I rarely buy anything from those companies.
- Why am I still signed up for newsletters I don't read?
  - Hmm. I don't know. Good point. I should do something about that.

3. Brainstorm Solutions

- Manually delete each email
- Use email automation – write an email deletion rule
- Pay someone to organize my emails
- Unsubscribe from one newsletter a day
- Delete all of my emails and start from scratch
- Open a new email account – completely start over

4. Weigh Pros and Cons of Solutions

- Manually delete each email
  - Pros – I'll see the email newsletters I've subscribed to
  - Cons – time consuming; I'm not interested in reading the newsletters
- Use email automation – write an email deletion rule
  - Pros – emails will be automatically deleted
  - Cons – I need to research how to create an email rule; there is a learning curve
- Pay someone to organize my emails
  - Pros – I don't have to do it
  - Cons – expensive; I have to give someone else access to my email account
- Unsubscribe from one newsletter a day
  - Pros – I won't receive any more unwanted emails

- o Cons – time consuming
- Delete all of my emails and start from scratch
  - o Pros – quick process
  - o Cons – I may accidentally delete emails I want to read or keep
- Open a new email account – completely start over
  - o Pros – start with a clean slate
  - o Cons – I'll have to re-subscribe to emails and newsletters that I want; I'll have to tell everyone my new email address; I'll have to periodically check my old email to make sure I don't miss anything

5. Rank Solutions

1. Use email automation – write an email deletion rule
2. Unsubscribe from one newsletter a day
3. Pay someone to organize my emails
4. Manually delete each email
5. Delete all of my emails and start from scratch
6. Open a new email account – completely start over

6. Evaluate Top Solutions

1. Use email automation – write an email deletion rule
   - o Immediate solution
   - o Works long term
   - o Gets me to a place where my inbox is more organized
2. Unsubscribe from one newsletter a day
   - o Long term solution
   - o Ensures I don't receive more unwanted email newsletters

7. Focus and Implement One Solution at a Time

- First, learn to write an email deletion rule and implement the rule in my inbox
- Second, unsubscribe from one email newsletter each day

8. Iterate and Reiterate

- Keep unsubscribing from unwanted emails
- Keep creating new email automation rules to unclutter my inbox
- Manually delete emails that the email rules do not delete

9. Keep Time in Mind

- 15 Minutes
  - Time it took to complete the exercise OR
  - Time limit set to complete the exercise

Now it's your turn. Use these steps to organize anything.

BONUS:
A BLANK CHECKLIST FOR YOUR OTHER "TO DOS"

LET'S DO THIS CHECKLIST

WEEK _____ DATE _____

- ❑ _____
- ❑ _____
- ❑ _____
- ❑ _____
- ❑ _____
- ❑ _____
- ❑ _____
- ❑ _____

NOTES _____

_____

WEEK _____ DATE _____

- ❑ _____
- ❑ _____
- ❑ _____
- ❑ _____
- ❑ _____
- ❑ _____
- ❑ _____
- ❑ _____

NOTES _____

_____

WEEK _____ **DATE** _____

- ☐ _____
- ☐ _____
- ☐ _____
- ☐ _____
- ☐ _____
- ☐ _____
- ☐ _____
- ☐ _____

NOTES _____

_____

WEEK _____ **DATE** _____

- ☐ _____
- ☐ _____
- ☐ _____
- ☐ _____
- ☐ _____
- ☐ _____
- ☐ _____
- ☐ _____

NOTES _____

_____

IMPORTANT INFORMATION AND RESOURCES
DOWNLOAD CHECKLISTS AND FORMS

Thank you for purchasing my book! Would you like to complete the checklists and forms during your move? Go here (https://tinyurl.com/p2krr54x) to download an interactive PDF containing the Order Your Life Moving Checklist, People to Notify When I Move Checklist, Order Your Life Apartment and House Hunting Checklist, Order Your Life High Value Inventory Form, Order Your Life Move In/Out Inspection Form, and the Let's Do This Checklist.

If you have trouble downloading the file, send an email to

hello@orderyourlife.com.

GET EARLY ACCESS TO THE LATEST CONTENT

Would you like early access to the latest Order Your Life content? Join our community at OrderYourLife.com. To get 10% off your moving kit, sign up here (https://tinyurl.com/4j9u9xzt).

CONNECT ON SOCIAL MEDIA

Facebook
   https://www.facebook.com/OrderYourLifeLLC
Twitter
   https://twitter.com/OrderYour_Life
Pinterest
   https://www.pinterest.com/OrderYour_Life
YouTube
   https://www.youtube.com/@orderyourlife
Blog
   https://orderyourlife.com/blogs/blog

REVIEW THIS BOOK

What did you think of this book? Your honest review is appreciated.

Please let others know what you think about the *Order Your Life Moving Guide*. Your opinion matters, and I greatly appreciate your honest review. Thank you!